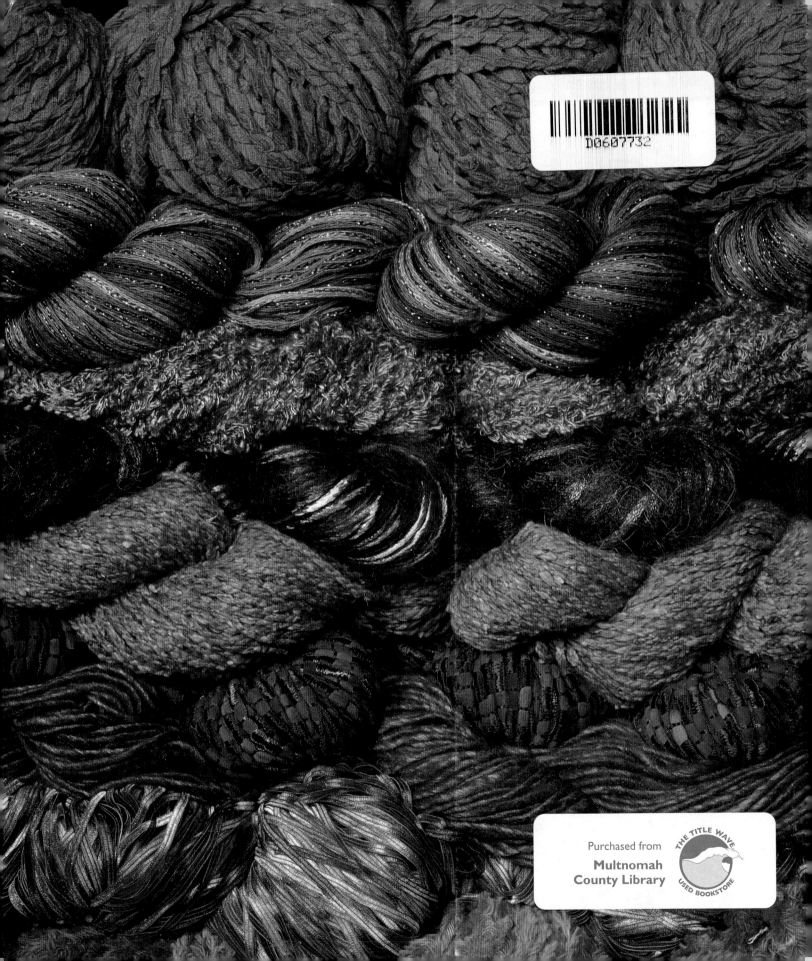

Tricoter

KNITTED THROWS

and More for the

SIMPLY BEAUTIFUL HOME

LINDEN PHELPS AND BERYL HIATT

Martingale™
& COMPANY

Knitted Throws and More for the Simply Beautiful Home
© 2002 by Linden Phelps and Beryl Hiatt

Martingale
& COMPANY

Martingale & Company
20205 144th Avenue NE
Woodinville, WA 98072-8478
www.martingale-pub.com

CREDITS

President . . . . Nancy J. Martin
CEO . . . . Daniel J. Martin
Publisher . . . . Jane Hamada
Editorial Director . . . . Mary V. Green
Managing Editor . . . . Tina Cook
Technical Editor . . . . Ursula Reikes
Copy Editor . . . . Karen Koll
Design Director . . . . Stan Green
Illustrator . . . . Robin Strobel
Photographer . . . . Brent Kane
Cover and Text Designers . . . . Stan Green
Jennifer LaRock Shontz

Printed in Hong Kong
07 06 05 04 03 02   8 7 6 5 4 3 2 1

Library of Congress Cataloging-in-Publication Data

Phelps, Linden.
    Knitted throws and more for the simply beautiful home / Linden Phelps and Beryl Hiatt.
        p. cm.
    ISBN 1-56477-421-X
    1. Knitting—Patterns. 2. Textile fabrics in interior decoration. I. Hiatt, Beryl. II. Title.
    TT835 .P35235 2002
    746.43 '2043—dc21   2002007622

MISSION STATEMENT

We are dedicated to providing quality products and service by working together to inspire creativity and to enrich the lives we touch.

THE THREAD OF LIFE

Our store is a very colorful, bustling, joyful place on any given day. Tables are usually filled with knitters engaged in their individual projects and in conversation with each other. Tricoter is a place where people gather—in good times to share their news and in troubling times to find comfort and support, oftentimes from someone who has gone through similar trials.

The power of knitting is frequently underestimated, viewed as something your grandmother may have taught you as a child or as a short-lived interest from a home-economics class, but not as part of modern life.

We have found that, much like religion in an odd way, knitting is a source of comfort for many people when their lives are in turmoil. The sense of fulfillment that comes from the actual process of creating something beautiful inspires one to continue long after the crisis has past.

Babies are completely awed and stimulated by the bright colors in our shop, so we're often joined by moms who come to knit knowing their babies are effortlessly entertained by the environment here. We keep a cookie jar filled with dog treats, so we're a favorite stop on many daily walks and have a number of canine customers who sleep quietly under tables while their owners knit.

In the hours following the devastation of September 11, 2001, our store became a safe haven of sorts, a place where a number of people gravitated. Conversation was hushed or nonexistent, but many of our customers automatically turned to the rhythmic process of knitting in order to cope with the horror of the day's events.

We dedicate this book to the process of knitting: To the calming, comforting, healing effects that occur as we reach without conscious thought to the needles that are never far from us. I know of no scientific evidence that knitting can change the world, but we have found that in even the most troubled times, knitting has helped to strengthen the fabric of our lives, a stitch at a time.

—Lindy

BACK ROW (left to right): Dinny Brones, Elizabeth Elmer, Blaise Wrenn, Beryl Hiatt, Ola Sankiewicz, Julie Harris. CENTER: Yiming Zhi. FRONT ROW (left to right): Rose Mueller, Stacy O'Hara, Roxanne Gallagher, Lindy Phelps. NOT PICTURED: Carol Simmons, Tanya Parieaux

We gratefully acknowledge our very talented Tricoter staff for their help with pattern support, sample knitting, and the beautiful finishing of our samples.

We would like to thank our technical editor, Ursula Reikes, for her amazing precision and patience and our photographer, Brent Kane, for his unfailing humor and for his unique skill that brought our ideas into such clear focus.

We thank the following friends who graciously opened their homes (and boat) to us to use as backdrops for the photography in this book: Jerry and Sybil Raine, Patrick Orton, Holly Henderson, the Clough family, and Beverly Elmer. Our thanks also to the Center for Wooden Boats in Seattle and particularly Captain Jim Flury and his beautiful *Wanderbird*.

Our Tricoter World

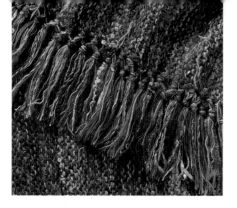

CONTENTS

THE SIMPLY BEAUTIFUL HOME

As we begin our third book, it has occurred to both of us how truly lucky we are that anyone wants to read about the thing in life that brings us the most joy! We certainly never saw ourselves as authors—we're just a couple of girls that love to knit, garden, and cook! The very fact that you're reading this is an indication that we're not alone in our desire to incorporate color, texture, and a love of great food into all aspects of our lives.

Our first two books, *Simply Beautiful Sweaters* and *Simply Beautiful Sweaters for Men,* are collections of some of our favorite sweaters. It seemed logical to us, when the topic turned to "the next book," that we would focus on what we love most—our homes.

For both of us, our homes are our private escapes from the busy, bustling atmosphere of our shop. As much as we both love the excitement and ever-changing energy that seems to radiate through Tricoter, we are nourished and renewed most by the environments that we have created in our homes.

Sunlit trees enliven a good walk.

We have to laugh when people assume that we love our shop because we get to knit all day. Nothing could be farther from the truth! Our shop is so busy, and there is so much required to keep it looking beautiful, that we rarely if ever get to pick up a pair of needles, let alone knit, other than to demonstrate a stitch to a customer. Our payoff is getting to go home and knit each evening.

We're both morning people. We're generally up at sunrise, getting a sprinkler going or fertilizing a few pots before we sit and knit for an hour or so while we enjoy our first latte of the day. It's also the time we organize our day—planning

Buds and blooms glow with rich color.

Produce stalls at the public market provide
colorful inspiration.

Living, as we do, in the Pacific Northwest, surrounded by the incredible beauty of the Olympic and Cascade Mountains as well as Lake Washington, Lake Union, and Puget Sound, we cannot help making time to get out and enjoy the natural beauty of our environment. We take long aerobic walks together several times a week. In addition to the obvious health benefits, this is our brainstorming time. Many of the projects that you see in this book were designed while we walked. The beauty of nature is a source of inspiration that cannot be overestimated.

It is our goal in this book, to share some of our favorite things. First and foremost, throws and pillows. These are the elements that soften and define our personal spaces—and those of our friends. We've also included some of our favorite recipes for simple, easy, very fresh food. And we have photographed our book in some of our favorite places: our homes, our gardens, and those of our friends. We hope that you will find our book enjoyable. May it inspire you to find the same joy in your environment that we have in ours.

dinner, setting the table for a small dinner party that evening, or whipping up a quick pastry crust for a fruit tart. We often call each other and arrange to meet on the way to work at the public market down on the waterfront. Here, we can pick up the freshest produce from local farmers, or seafood just in from the fishing boats that morning.

The realization we have both come to is that great food doesn't have to be complicated or time-consuming to prepare. Our favorite meals consist of the very freshest ingredients, simply prepared and beautifully presented.

Because our lives are so busy, we are constantly looking for ways to streamline our food, our gardens, and even our knitting. We don't want to sacrifice one bit of the beauty or joy—we *do* want to make certain we've found the most efficient and effective method for "having it all."

A Northwest sunset wraps the landscape
in purples and pinks.

GETTING STARTED

KNITTING YOUR SWATCH

This is the most creative part of knitting. We're always surprised to hear customers complain about taking the time to knit a swatch. For us, it is the most exciting point: feeling the yarn, finding out what works, learning how certain stitches show off the beauty of a particular yarn while others get lost in the texture or color, deciding what needle size makes the yarn look and feel best, and discovering what colors work—or don't work—next to others.

Combinations that look beautiful together on a tray may have a different feel when knit in various combinations. Knitting swatches is your opportunity to play with color. Cast on twenty stitches or so, and don't be afraid to try unusual combinations or add a color that you normally wouldn't consider. A good friend and avid gardener once reminded us that color in knitting is no different than in a garden. While you would probably never plant a whole garden of marigolds, the accent that they add when combined with the colorful palette of spring flowers brings all of the colors to life.

Your swatch is also your opportunity to explore new ground, to experiment outside your comfort zone. There is very little lost over twenty stitches. It is much less painful than tearing out 8" of painstaking knitting on a project when you realize that the total color repeat you selected doesn't look the way you envisioned. Swatching is your chance to explore new stitches, to test new techniques. Find out what kinds of stitches you enjoy working with and which ones are too confusing or difficult to execute on the yarns you've chosen. As a rule, cotton and linen yarns have very little give, whereas wool, cashmere, and many blends

are much more pliable or forgiving. It is important not to "force" a swatch (by stretching or squishing it) just to get a gauge. Remember that when it all comes together it will look and feel right to you. If this isn't happening after a few tries, add a new yarn, or try a different stitch, or change needle size, or put it down and look for a different idea altogether. It is important to love your swatch first. If you burn out on the swatch, you can be sure that you won't enjoy knitting a whole project based on it.

One of the most frustrating comments we hear is "I stopped knitting because nothing I knit ever turned out the way it was supposed to—it never looked right." While knitting is not an exact science, it certainly shouldn't be a random shot in the dark either. When you approach it with some basic tools, it is an easy-to-estimate and simple-to-adjust process. Knitting a swatch to determine your gauge is the first critical step.

DETERMINING YOUR GAUGE

Gauge, or tension, is the most important factor in creating finished projects that match your initial concept in size and appearance. All patterns are based on a specific number of stitches and rows per inch. If your knitting does not match those specifications, your finished project will not turn out as you had hoped.

To determine gauge, knit a sample swatch at least 4" wide and 4" long with the yarn and needles you will use for your project. Because the stitches at the end of the knitting tend to be somewhat distorted, you'll want to measure at least 1 stitch in from the selvage edges of the swatch. Therefore, cast on at least 2 more stitches than needed to

make 4" of measurable knitting. Work the pattern stitch specified to check the gauge; if no pattern is given, work the swatch in stockinette stitch. If the pattern is complex (color work or lace), work a larger swatch, perhaps 6" to 8" square.

To measure the swatch, lay it flat. Place a tape measure parallel to a row of stitches and count the number of stitches (including fractions of inches) that make 4". Divide the number of stitches in the 4" swatch by 4 to get the number of stitches per inch. This is your gauge.

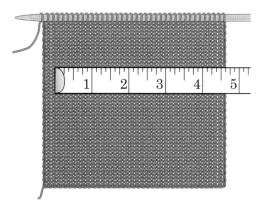

Compare the gauge to that specified in your pattern. If your swatch has too few stitches, your work is too loose; try again with smaller needles. If your swatch has too many stitches, your work is too tight; try larger needles or a different yarn. You are ready to begin knitting when your gauge matches that specified by the pattern.

The gauge swatch may be saved or pulled out and reused. You can bind off the stitches and use the swatch to test the washability and colorfastness of the yarn(s), or save it in a notebook with other swatches for future reference.

The next step is to take your gauge (the number of stitches per inch) and multiply that by the width in inches you want your finished project to measure. As you knit, lay your work flat. Without stretching it, measure every few inches to see if your gauge has changed. When knitting on straight needles, it is important to stop halfway across the row so you can lay your work out completely flat to measure it.

Continue to measure both the length and width of the piece as you knit. It is not uncommon for your gauge to change significantly due to increased stress, fatigue, or lack of concentration. It is relatively simple to adjust your pattern, increasing or decreasing a couple of stitches at this point. This is a habit that you should get used to and continue to practice throughout all of your knitting.

SUBSTITUTING YARNS

If you're interested in using a yarn other than one specified in the project directions, remember that the most important thing is to select a yarn or yarns that knit at the same gauge. This can be determined only by swatching. Depending on the yarn or combination of yarns you select, you may want to go up or down a needle size to get the specified gauge. Don't be afraid to experiment with your swatch to make certain that you are happy with the look and feel of the swatch before you proceed. This step is very much like cooking: experimentation very often leads to an even better product.

KNITTING TERMS AND ABBREVIATIONS

BC (bc)	back cross		**P**	purl
beg	begin(ning)		**patt**	pattern
BO	bind off		**PSSO**	pass slipped stitch(es) over
C#B	cable # stitches to the back		**rep**	repeat
C#F	cable # stitches to the front		**rib**	ribbing
ch	chain		**RS**	right side
CO	cast on		**sc**	single crochet
cont	continue		**seed st**	seed stitch
dec	decrease		**SBC**	single back cross
dpn	double-pointed needle		**SFC**	single front cross
FC (fc)	front cross		**SSK**	slip, slip, knit
garter st	garter stitch		**st(s)**	stitch(es)
inc	increase		**St st**	stockinette stitch
K	knit		**sl**	slip as if to purl unless otherwise noted
K2tog	knit two together		**WS**	wrong side
M1	make one stitch		**YO**	yarn over

SLEEK SOPHISTICATION

Our friend Sybil's home is so serenely beautiful yet seductively sensuous that it provided the perfect backdrop for our luxurious, fur-trimmed throw. A sculptor, Sybil manages to take the very coldest and hardest of mediums—limestone and marble—and create incredibly sensuous figures whose stunning simplicity and soft beauty seem to mock the very materials from which they are made. We designed this throw for Sybil as a soft, sumptuous contrast to the rich, saturated colors and sophisticated textures that form her personal environment. Simple, healthy pasta and a glass of wine are perfect for the informal entertaining that Sybil enjoys.

Size: 42" x 52"

MATERIALS

Use a very chunky yarn or a combination of smaller yarns that knits at 2.5 sts to 1".

4 skeins Filatura di Crosa Ritratto, color 14 (approx. 198 yds/skein)

9 skeins S. Charles Collezione Mosaic, color 105 (approx. 99 yds/skein)

10 skeins Trendsetter Metal, color 57 (approx. 85 yds/skein)

7 skeins Prism Flash in Embers (approx. 125 yds/skein)

3 skeins Filatura di Crosa Baby Kid Extra, color 469 (approx. 268 yds/skein)

6 skeins GGH Cometa, color 003 (approx. 50 yds/skein) for trim

1 yard faux fur for edging

#15 circular needles (47")

Size G crochet hook

GAUGE

10 sts and 12 rows = 4" in patt

Always check gauge before starting project. Increase or decrease needle size to obtain correct gauge.

MISTAKE RIB PATTERN STITCH

Patt rep is an uneven multiple of 3 sts.

NOTE: This pattern does not have edge stitches.

Every row: K2, P1 across the row, ending with P1.

DIRECTIONS

1. With 5 yarns held together as one, CO 105 sts. Work in mistake rib patt stitch until work measures 52" from beg of work.
2. BO loosely.

FINISHING

1. With Cometa, work 1 row sc around all 4 sides of throw.

2. Create a framework through which the faux fur will be threaded as follows:
   - ▶ With Cometa and size G crochet hook, work 1 sc on RS in one corner of throw. Ch 7, connect seventh ch with sc in second st in from edge, about 1½" farther along edge of throw on RS.
   - ▶ Fold over edge to work sts on WS. Work 1 sc on WS in the same place where you connected last ch, ch 7 and connect seventh ch with sc in second st in from edge about 1½" farther along same edge on WS.
   - ▶ Cont in this manner, alternating from RS to WS around the 4 sides of throw.

3. Cut faux fur into 3"-wide strips, aligning pelt lines if there are obvious ones. You will need enough strips to yield 16 feet of fur when joined.

4. With RS facing, sew strips together end to end. Fold long strip of faux fur in half lengthwise and sew 2 edges together as close to edge as possible.

5. Turn faux fur RS out and thread through crochet edge.

TIP

Both Beryl and I wanted to knit this throw, and we prefer straight needles to circulars. So we knit it in two sections (CO 52 sts each) on straight needles and joined the strips together with a center vertical seam. This is a great idea for those who travel and don't want to carry along such a large piece. —Lindy

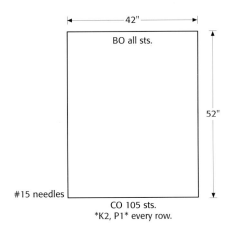

42"

BO all sts.

52"

#15 needles

CO 105 sts.
K2, P1 every row.

ROASTED ASPARAGUS WITH ORZO

I have always loved the flavor of vegetables that are oven roasted. This easy "one-dish dinner" pairs roasted asparagus with the creamy texture of orzo. I have experimented with a number of variations over the years; roasted green beans work very well if asparagus is not available. —Lindy

INGREDIENTS

1½ cups chicken stock

2 tablespoons olive oil

5 cloves garlic, sliced

2 bunches asparagus, washed and cut on diagonal into 2" pieces

1 pound orzo pasta

⅔ cup pine nuts, toasted

¼ cup Parmesan Reggiano cheese, shredded

¼ cup Parmesan Reggiano cheese, shaved

Salt and pepper to taste

DIRECTIONS

1. Preheat oven to 450°. Bring water for pasta to a boil.
2. Meanwhile, simmer chicken stock over medium heat until reduced by about half.
3. Place olive oil and sliced garlic in the bottom of a shallow roasting pan; heat in oven until oil begins to sizzle.
4. Add asparagus and roast, tossing frequently, for about 8 to 10 minutes or until tender but not soft.
5. While asparagus is roasting, cook orzo to al dente stage (tender but still firm to bite); drain.
6. Add reduced chicken stock, orzo, pine nuts, and shredded Parmesan Reggiano to roasting pan and toss with asparagus and garlic. Salt and pepper to taste.
7. Serve topped with shaved cheese.

Serves 4.

SOFT IMPRESSIONS

Beryl's home is a reflection of her passion for beauty, color, and texture. Between riotous splashes of living color in the myriad pots that line the deck overlooking Lake Washington, and the kaleidoscopic collection of vividly colored ceramics and glass that Beryl collects, there are no dull or bare surfaces upon which to gaze. Her fiancé's influence is evident in the more serene Asian influences that provide a soothing balance. The throw she designed to complete their home combines a blend of soft chenille and mohair fibers accented with hand-dyed silk ribbon. Curling up under this cozy throw in front of a fire while enjoying warm cobbler right from the oven on a crisp evening is a perfect way to end the day.

Size: 48" x 60"

MATERIALS

Use a very chunky yarn or combination of smaller yarns that knits at 2.0 sts to 1".

12 skeins Trendsetter Dune, color 30 (approx. 90 yds/skein)

9 skeins Colinette Isis in velvet gold 112 (approx. 110 yds/skein)

9 skeins Noro Cashmel, color 11 (approx. 105 yds/skein)

17½ yds. Hanah Silk 2½"-wide silk charmeuse ribbon in Liquid Amber for trim

#17 circular needles (47")

GAUGE

8.0 sts and 16 rows = 4" in St st

Always check gauge before starting project. Increase or decrease needle size to obtain correct gauge.

PATTERN STITCHES
PATTERN A

Patt rep is 16 plus 8 plus 1.

NOTE: Inc by knitting into front and back of same stitch.

Row 1 (RS): K4, *K1, inc 1 in next st, K5, sl 1, K2tog, PSSO, K5, inc 1 in next st*, rep from * to * 5 more times, end K5.

Row 2: K4, P across row, end K4.

Rep rows 1 and 2 until work measures 10", ending on WS row.

PATTERN B

Row 1 (RS): Knit.
Row 2: Knit.
Row 3: Knit.
Row 4: Knit.
Row 5: K5, *YO, K2tog*, rep from * to * across row, end K4.
Row 6: Knit.
Rows 7–14: Rep rows 3–6 twice.
Rows 15 and 16: Knit.

DIRECTIONS

1. With all 3 yarns held together as one, CO 105 sts. Work 7 rows in garter st, ending on WS row.
2. Work patt A followed by patt B, 3 times.
3. Rep patt A only, 1 more time.
4. Work 8 rows of garter st. BO all sts.

TIP

This is a project that proves the point that it's always good to have several projects going at one time. Beryl loved knitting this throw when she was not stressed and could enjoy the rhythm of the pattern itself. But on late evenings, when she wanted the mindless comfort of knitting without having to concentrate, she found that this was not the right project, because she wound up making mistakes. It was then that she turned to a less involved project.

—Lindy

FINISHING

Thread silk ribbon through holes created by patt B at intervals throughout throw as shown. Tack as needed to avoid slippage.

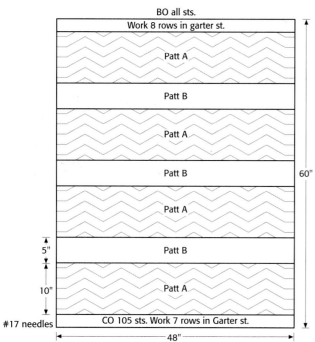

BO all sts.
Work 8 rows in garter st.

Patt A

Patt B

Patt A

Patt B

Patt A

Patt B

Patt A

CO 105 sts. Work 7 rows in Garter st.

60"

5"

10"

#17 needles

48"

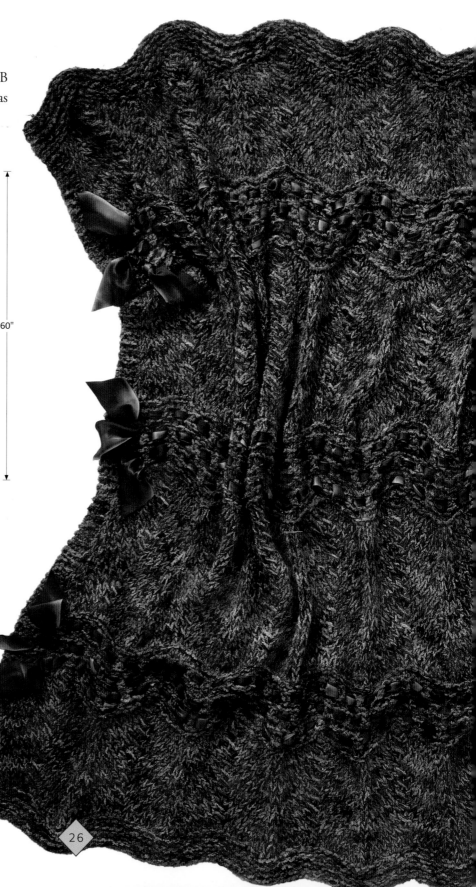

PEACH AND NECTARINE COBBLER

Beryl grew up with a mother who loved to cook, so her talent for this type of "comfort food" came naturally to her. We have explored many versions of fruit cobblers, pies, tarts, etc., but this is the standard by which the others are ultimately judged! —Lindy

CRUST INGREDIENTS

2 cups unbleached flour

1 cup whole wheat flour

¾ teaspoon salt

1 tablespoon baking powder

3 tablespoons plus 2 tablespoons granulated sugar

9 tablespoons cold butter, plus enough to butter pie pan

9 tablespoons vegetable shortening (Crisco)

¾ cup whole milk

1 egg yolk

2 tablespoons half-and-half

FILLING INGREDIENTS

1½ pounds fresh, ripe peaches (3 large)

1½ pounds fresh, ripe nectarines (3 large)

2 tablespoons cornstarch

⅔ cup granulated sugar

¼ teaspoon freshly grated nutmeg

1 teaspoon ground cinnamon

2 tablespoons vanilla

Juice and zest of 1 large lemon

DIRECTIONS

1. Preheat oven to 400°. Butter 11"-diameter deep-dish pie pan (ceramic or glass).

2. In a large mixing bowl, combine flours, salt, baking powder, and 3 tablespoons sugar; mix well.

3. Cut butter and shortening into ¼" pieces and add to dry mixture, tossing to coat. Using a pastry cutter, cut in butter and shortening, being careful not to over-manipulate dough. (We *don't* recommend a food processor, because no matter how little we pulse to mix, the dough comes out tough.)

4. Add milk and blend with a rubber spatula until combined but not smooth. Set aside.

5. In a large pot, bring water (enough to cover several pieces of fruit at a time) to a boil. Turn off heat.

6. Place fruit in boiling water for 30 seconds. (If floating, turn at 15 seconds.)

7. Remove carefully and peel skin under cold running water.

8. Pit; cut in generous slices.

9. In a second large mixing bowl, gently mix fruit with balance of filling ingredients.

10. Spoon filling into buttered pie pan. Place pie pan on a rimmed baking sheet (in the event that topping bubbles over while cooking).

11. Bake for 15 minutes and remove to add topping.

12. Spoon dough a tablespoon at a time and cover filling, flattening each piece slightly. (Handle dough as little as possible to avoid a tough crust.)

13. In a small bowl, whisk egg yolk slightly, add half-and-half, and brush topping with mixture. Sprinkle with 2 tablespoons of sugar.

14. Return to oven and bake until filling is bubbly and topping is golden (about 30 minutes).

Cool for at least 10 minutes. Serve while still warm. It's *great* with vanilla ice cream!

Serves 6–8.

NATURALLY NEUTRAL

Lindy's environment in a classic 1904 Craftsman duplex has the distinct feel of a European pied-à-terre. High ceilings, large bay windows that overlook a lush, private garden, and an eclectic collection of furniture, art, and accessories form the backdrop for this beautiful throw. Perfectly scaled for her delicate French settees, this combination of cashmere, silk, mohair, and a variety of soft, silky fibers have made this a Tricoter favorite. The kitchen with its original glass-doored cabinets, copper and wood counters, and collection of copper pots overhead seems often to be the place where everyone gathers despite its limited size. The recipe for salmon in parchment with the surprise of the wasabe cream is one of her favorites for easy weeknight entertaining when prep time is limited.

Size: 48" x 60"

MATERIALS

Use a very chunky yarn or combination of
  smaller yarns that knits at 2.16 sts to 1".
14 skeins Trendsetter Dune, color 76
  (approx. 90 yds/skein)
10 skeins Ironstone Desert Flower, color 6
  (approx. 126 yds/skein)
8 skeins Trendsetter Bollicina, color 7 (approx. 145
  yds/skein)
6 skeins Lang Opal, color 0026 (approx. 170 yds/skein)
10 yds. Hanah Silk, 2½"-wide silk charmeuse hand-dyed
  ribbon
#17 circular, needles (47")
Size N crochet hook

GAUGE

8.65 sts and 10 rows = 4" in St st
Always check gauge before starting project. Increase or
  decrease needle size to obtain correct gauge.

DIRECTIONS

1. With all 4 yarns held together, CO 102 sts and set up
   patt as follows:

   Row 1 (RS): K1 (edge st), *K5, P5*, rep from * to *,
     end K1 (edge st).

   Row 2 and all even-numbered rows: Work sts as they
     face you.

   Row 3: K1, P1, *K5, P5*, rep from * to *, end K1.
   Row 5: K1, P2, *K5, P5*, rep from * to *, end K1.
   Row 7: K1, P3, *K5, P5*, rep from * to *, end K1.
   Row 9: K1, P4, *K5, P5*, rep from * to *, end K1.
   Row 11: K1, P5, *K5, P5*, rep from * to *, end K1.
   Row 13: K1, K1, P5, *K5, P5*, rep from * to *, end K1.
   Row 15: K1, K2, P5, *K5, P5*, rep from * to *, end K1.
   Row 17: K1, K3, P5, *K5, P5*, rep from * to *, end K1.
   Row 19: K1, K4, P5, *K5, P5*, rep from * to *, end K1.

Row 20: Work sts as they face you.

Rep rows 1–20.

NOTE: Because you are moving the pattern 1 stitch to the right on every right-side row, you will not end every row with a complete pattern repeat.

2. When work measures approximately 60" from bottom of work (lay flat to measure), BO all sts.

FINISHING

1. With all 4 yarns held together, work 1 row sc around all 4 sides of throw, followed by a row of crab stitch (see page 88).

2. Use remaining Trendsetter Dune, Ironstone Desert Flower, and Trendsetter Bollicina for fringe. Referring to "Fringe" on page 93, cut 10" fringe and attach along top and bottom of throw. Create "sneezes" (see page 93) with your trimmings and attach them with 6" pieces of 2½"-wide silk or satin ribbon at 4" intervals along top and bottom of throw as shown.

TIP

Mark the RS of your work with a piece of yarn or ribbon to remind you that the RS is the side on which you move the pattern. Because both sides are the same, it's easy to forget which is the right or wrong side without some kind of marker.

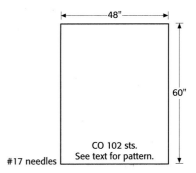

48"

60"

CO 102 sts.
See text for pattern.

#17 needles

SALMON IN PARCHMENT WITH WASABI CREAM

We get great salmon here in the Pacific Northwest. It's a bonus for us that it's also one of the healthiest foods imaginable! This is a recipe that we often use when entertaining because it's easy to prepare ahead and makes a beautiful presentation in addition to tasting great. Once you try the wasabi cream you'll be looking for other ways to use it.

DIRECTIONS

1. Preheat oven to 350°.
2. Place half of chopped shallots in center of each piece of parchment.
3. Place fillets over bed of chopped shallots and top each with ½ tablespoon butter. Sprinkle each fillet with ½ teaspoon herbs and salt and pepper.
4. Seal parchment around fish and crimp edges to secure, leaving air space around each fillet.
5. Place in shallow roasting pan. Bake for 30 minutes.
6. Mix the wasabi powder and water in a small bowl until a smooth paste is achieved.
7. Whip cream until it forms smooth peaks.
8. Fold wasabi paste and salt into whipped cream.
9. Remove salmon fillets from parchment, top with a heaping tablespoon of wasabi cream, and serve.

Serves 2.

INGREDIENTS

4 to 6 shallots, peeled and finely chopped
2 sheets parchment, each approximately 16" long
Two King salmon fillets, approximately ½ pound each
1 tablespoon butter
1 teaspoon herbes de Provence*
Salt and pepper to taste
3 tablespoons wasabi powder (or to taste)
3 tablespoons water
¼ cup whipping cream
Generous pinch of salt

A delightful blend of rosemary, basil, marjoram, savory, and thyme

THE MEN'S CLUB

Our very dear friend Patrick's background in fine art is evident in his home. A Renaissance man with a history in far too many fields to keep track of, he has always chosen simplicity and serenity for his private space. We designed a throw for Patrick that combines classic cables in a collection of natural fibers that shed minimally and give a masculine yet cozy feel to his elegantly spare environment. Perfectly grilled chops with fresh lemon and olive oil, the freshest vegetables, of the season, and a glass of great red wine form one of Patrick's favorite meals.

Size: 48" x 60"

MATERIALS

Use a chunky yarn or combination of smaller yarns that
knits at 3.0 sts to 1".

10 skeins Rowan Felted Tweed, color 138
(approx. 190 yds/skein.)

16 skeins Rowan Wool Cotton, color 930
(approx. 123 yds/skein)

18 skeins Gedifra Kid Royal, color 1204
(approx. 110 yds/skein)

5 yds. bronze Mokuba patent leather cording
(to wrap tassels)*

#15 circular needles (47")

Large cable needle or dpn (see "Tip," page 00)

* If leather is unavailable, use a thin suede cord or yarn.

GAUGE

12 sts and 18 rows = 4" in patt

Always check gauge before starting project. Increase or
decrease needle size to obtain correct gauge.

SEED STITCH

Row 1: *K1, P1*; rep from * to *.

Row 2: Purl the knit sts and knit the purl sts as they face
you.

Rep rows 1–2.

TIP

When working on large cables like in the Men's
Club, we find that 7" double-pointed needles
are an excellent alternative to traditional cable
needles.

DIRECTIONS

1. With all 3 yarns held together as one, CO 146 sts.

2. **Rows 1–89 (except those listed below):** K1, work 16
   sts in St st, *work 16 sts in seed st, work 16 sts in St st*,
   rep from * to * across, end K1. (This includes edge sts.)

   Rows 15, 45, 75: Work cable twists as follows: K1,
   C8B, K8, *work 16 sts in seed st, C8B, K8*, rep from *
   to * across row, K1.

3. **Rows 90–179 (except those listed below):** Switching
   the order of the St st and seed st, work panels as follows:
   K1, work 16 sts in seed st, *work 16 sts in St st, work
   16 sts in seed st*, rep from * to * across row, end K1.

   Rows 105, 135, 165: Work cable twists as follows:
   K1, work 16 sts in seed st, *C8B, K8, work 16 sts in
   seed st*, rep from * to * across row, end K1.

4. **Rows 180–269:** As rows 1–89.

   Rows 195, 225, and 255: Work cable twists as
   on row 15.

5. BO all sts on row 270.

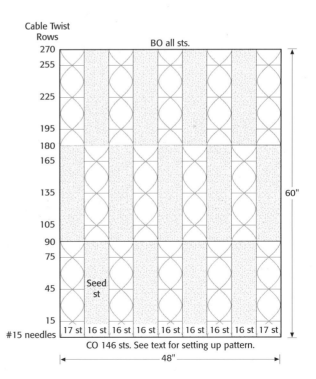

FINISHING

Make ten 3"-long chubby tassels and ten twisted cords using the remaining yarns. Wrap tassels with patent leather cord. Attach tassels with twisted cords at each end of the throw, placing one at the center of each cable. See "Tassels" and "Twisted Cords" on pages 91–92.

COUNTRY-STYLE PORK CHOPS WITH LEMON AND OLIVE OIL

Our first trip to Italy convinced us that great food doesn't have to be complicated or difficult to prepare.
This very simple recipe makes the best pork chops we've ever tasted! A steamed vegetable
and roasted potatoes make this one of the best meals imaginable!

INGREDIENTS

2 pork loin chops, 1" thick with bone in
1 large (or 2 small) lemons, halved
2 tablespoons olive oil
Salt and pepper to taste

DIRECTIONS

1. Generously salt and pepper both sides of chops.
2. Grill or broil pork chops over high heat, approximately 5 to 7 minutes per side.
3. Remove from heat and immediately squeeze the juice of ½ a lemon over each chop and drizzle with a tablespoon of olive oil to create a lovely sauce. Salt and pepper to taste.

Serves 2.

AFTERNOON DELIGHT

The setting for this throw epitomizes what we love most about our lives: the natural beauty of our surroundings here in Seattle, the joy found in sitting outside on a beautiful afternoon to indulge in our passion for knitting, and a delicious lunch close by. We're certain there can be no greater pleasure than this! We have been influenced a great deal over the years by the Missoni family. Their use of color and texture has fascinated us and inspired a number of our sweaters. This throw is a very graphic tribute to their well-known use of black and white played against vivid, clear colors.

Size: 36" x 60"

MATERIALS

Use a chunky yarn that knits at 3 sts to 1".

22 skeins of Horstia Mogador (approx. 99 yds/skein)

  4 skeins black 8 (A)

  3 skeins white 101 (B)

  3 skeins red 112 (C)

  3 skeins pink 116 (D)

  3 skeins purple 126 (E)

  2 skeins gold 104 (F)

  2 skeins orange 113 (G)

  2 skeins green 129 (H)

#10½ needles

Size J crochet hook

GAUGE

12 sts and 11 rows = 4" in St st

Always check gauge before starting project. Increase or
  decrease needle size to obtain correct gauge.

DIRECTIONS

The throw is knit in three 20" x 36" panels that are sewn
together.

PANEL 1 (MAKE 2)

 1. With color E, CO 66 sts and work 19 rows, beg on WS
    row, as follows:

    K1, P16, K16, P16, K17. On every other row, work sts
      as they face you to create blocks of St st and rev St st.

 2. Switch to color A and work color break as follows:

    Row 1 (RS): K1, P16, K16, P16, K17.

    Row 2: K17, P16, K16, P16, K1.

 3. Switch to color C and work 20 rows, beg on RS row, as
    follows:

    K17, P16, K16, P16, K1. On every other row, work sts
      as they face you to create blocks of St st and rev St st.

 4. Switch to color A and work color break as follows:

    Row 1 (RS): K17, P16, K16, P16, K1.

    Row 2: K1, P16, K16, P16, K17.

5. Switch to color H and work 20 rows as in step 1.

6. Switch to color A and work color break as in step 2.

7. Switch to color D and work 20 rows as in step 3.

8. Switch to color A and work color break as in step 4.

9. Switch to color F and work 20 rows as in step 1.

10. Switch to color A and work color break as in step 2.

11. Switch to color G and work 19 rows as in step 3.

12. BO all sts on next row.

PANEL 2 (MAKE 1)

1. With color A, CO 98 sts. Set up color work as follows:

   Row 1 (RS): K1 with colors A and B, *P8 with A, K8 with B*, rep from * to * 4 times, end P8 with A, K9 with B.

   Row 2: K1 with B, *P8 with B, K8 with A*, rep from * to * 4 times, end P8 with B, K8 with A, K1 with A and B.

   Rows 3, 5, 7: Rep row 1.

   Rows 4, 6, 8: Rep row 2.

2. Switch to color A and work color break as follows:

   Row 1 (RS): K1, P16, *K16, P16*, rep from * to * once, end K17.

   Row 2: K17, *P16, K16*, rep from * to * once, end P16, K1.

NOTE: For garter-stitch breaks between each color, knit over knit sections and purl over purl sections as they face you on first row. On second row, purl over knit sections and knit over purl sections as they face you— this creates a uniform pattern of lines.

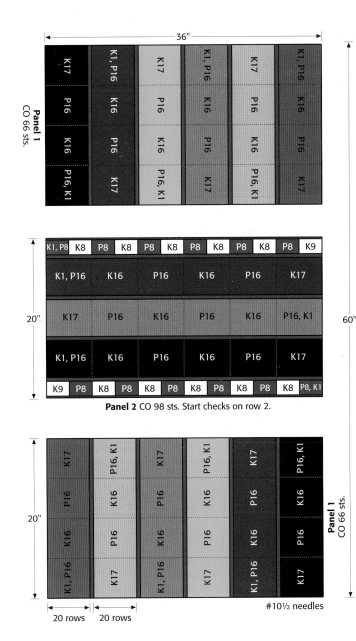

Panel 2 CO 98 sts. Start checks on row 2.

TIP

Whenever using black and/or white yarns with bright colors in a project, it is a good idea (even if the manufacturer specifies otherwise) to plan to dry-clean your project. Our experience has been that black yarns, and especially reds, very often bleed into white yarn, and black sometimes bleeds into bright colors.

3. Switch to color E and work 20 rows as follows:

K17, *P16, K16*, rep from * to * once, end P16, K1. On every other row, work sts as they face you to create blocks of St st and rev St st.

4. Switch to color A and work color break as follows:

Row 1 (RS): K17, *P16, K16*, rep from * to * once, end P16, K1.

Row 2: K1, P16, *K16, P16*, rep from * to * once, end K17.

5. Switch to color D and work 20 rows as follows:

K1, P16, *K16, P16*, rep from * to * once, end K17. On every other row, work sts as they face you to create blocks of St st and rev St st.

6. Switch to color A and work color break as in step 2.

7. Switch to color C and work 20 rows as step 3.

8. Switch to color A and work color break as in step 4.

9. Complete second color work border as follows:

Row 1 (RS): K1 with colors A and B, *K8 with B, P8 with A*, rep from * to * 4 times, end K8 with B, P8 with A, K1 with A.

Row 2: K9 with A, *P8 with B, K8 with A*, rep from * to * 4 times, end P8 B, K1 with A and B.

Rows 3, 5, 7: Rep row 1.

Rows 4, 6: Rep row 2.

Row 8: BO all sts with A.

FINISHING

1. With color A, work 1 row sc along both side edges of each panel 1 piece. Work 1 row sc along the CO and BO edges of panel 2.

2. Referring to the diagram on page 41, join the 3 panels with sl st crochet, referring to "Joining Crocheted Edges" on page 89. Remember to reverse the second of the 2 like panels so that the colors are in reverse order.

3. With equal amounts of colors A and B, create 4 twisted cords and 4 large tassels. See "Tassels" and "Twisted Cords" on pages 91–92. Attach tassels to corners of throw with twisted cord.

TUNA AND ARUGULA BAGUETTES

This is definitely not your grandmother's tuna sandwich! The combination of a great, hearty bread with tangy
olive tapenade spread, the nutty flavor of arugula, and the crunch of bell peppers, celery,
and capers in the tuna salad makes this truly a memorable meal.

INGREDIENTS

12-ounce can solid white tuna packed in water, drained
    and separated with a fork
1 stalk celery, chopped
2 scallions, chopped
¼ small yellow or orange bell pepper, seeded and chopped
2 tablespoons fresh cilantro, chopped
4 tablespoons light mayonnaise
1 tablespoon tarragon or Dijon mustard
1½ tablespoons capers, drained
1 tablespoon lemon juice
1 rustic baguette or 4 slices of rustic bread
6-ounce jar of black-olive tapenade
Fresh baby arugula leaves

DIRECTIONS

1. In a medium-size mixing bowl, combine tuna, celery,
   scallions, bell pepper, cilantro, mayonnaise, mustard,
   capers, and lemon juice and mix well.
2. Slice baguette lengthwise, toast lightly if desired, and
   spread the cut surface of top slice with a thin coating of
   olive tapenade. Add mayonnaise or butter if desired.
3. Place a layer of baby arugula leaves on bottom slice of
   baguette and top with tuna mixture.
4. Add top portion of baguette and slice crosswise into
   individual portions.

Serves 2.

SAIL AWAY

This throw was conceived last summer during the first annual knitting cruise. Our friend (and coworker) Elizabeth and her husband spend much of the summer on their fifty-foot sailboat up in the San Juan and Gulf Islands. At the end of the racing season and before the boat was brought back down to Seattle for the winter, Elizabeth invited another friend and me to spend a week sailing, knitting, and cooking. We spent our days up on deck enjoying the late summer weather and our evenings in the beautiful teak salon and galley, trading off the cooking responsibilities and knitting. The idea for this throw came from the nautical cable patterns which, like family crests, signified the families of Norwegian fishermen. (And they were often used to identify sailors drowned in the course of their trade.) The Center for Wooden Boats in Seattle kindly arranged for this throw to be photographed on the beautiful *Wanderbird*, which is moored there.

TIP

When knitting multiple repeats of patterns such as these, we like to make several photocopies of the pattern stitch. Then when we work each repeat we simply highlight each row on a photocopy as we work on it.

MATERIALS

Use a very chunky yarn or combination of smaller yarns that knits at 2.16 sts to 1".

36 skeins Filatura di Crosa Air Wool (approx. 55 yds/skein)
    24 skeins red 6
    12 skeins dark navy 5
14 yds. of 3mm gold braid (for trim only)
#13 circular needles (32")
#11 or #13 double-pointed needles
Large cable needle or dpn (see "Tip" on page 35)
Large tapestry needle

Size: 48" x 60"

GAUGE

8.65 sts and 9 rows = 4" in St st

Always check gauge before starting project.

Increase or decrease needle size to obtain correct gauge.

PATTERN STITCHES
PATTERN 1: NAUTICAL TWISTED ROPE (PANEL OF 49 STS)
Make 3.

NOTES:

Front Cross (FC): Sl 2 to dpn and hold in front, K2, then K2 from dpn.

Back Cross (BC): Sl 2 to dpn and hold in back, K2, then K2 from dpn.

M1: Pick up running thread before next st and purl into the back of this thread.

Row 1 (RS): (P2, K4) 4 times, P1, (K4, P2) 4 times.

Row 2, 4, 6, and 8: (K2, P4) 4 times, K1, (P4, K2) 4 times.

Row 3: (P2, FC, P2, K4) twice, P1 (K4, P2, BC, P2) twice.

Row 5: Rep row 1.

Row 7: P2, FC, P2, K4, P2, FC, P2, sl next 5 sts to dpn and hold in front, K4, sl the purl st from dpn back to left-hand needle and purl it, K4 from dpn, P2, BC, P2, K4, P2, BC, P2.

Row 9: P2, K4, P2, *M1, (K4, P2) twice, K4, M1*, P1, rep from * to *, end P2, K4, P2.

Row 10: K2, P4, *K3, P4, (K2, P4) twice*, rep from * to *, end K3, P4, K2.

Row 11: P2, FC, P3, M1, K4, P2tog, FC, P2tog, K4, M1, P3, M1, K4, P2tog, BC, P2tog, K4, M1, P3, BC, P2.

Row 12: K2, P4, K4, *(P4, K1) twice, P4*, K5, rep from * to *, end K4, P4, K2.

Row 13: P2, K4, P4, *M1, K3, SSK, K4, K2tog, K3, M1*, P5, rep from * to *, end P4, K4, P2.

Row 14: K2, P4, K5, P12, K7, P12, K5, P4, K2.

Row 15: P2, FC, P5, M1, K4, FC, K4, M1, P7, M1, K4, BC, K4, M1, P5, BC, P2.

Row 16: K2, P4, K6, P12, K9, P12, K6, P4, K2.

Row 17: P2, K4, P6, sl next 8 sts to dpn and hold to back, K4, then sl the second 4 sts from dpn back to left-hand needle and K them, K4 from dpn, P9, sl next 8 sts to dpn and hold to front, K4, then sl the second 4 sts from dpn back to left-hand needle and K them, K4 from dpn, P6, K4, P2.

Rows 18, 20, 22, and 24: Rep rows 16, 14, 12, and 10.

Row 19: P2, FC, P4, P2tog, K4, FC, K4, P2tog, P5, P2tog, K4, BC, K4, P2tog, P4, BC, P2.

Row 21: P2, K4, P3, *P2tog, (K4, M1) twice, K4, P2tog, P3*, rep from * to *, end K4, P2.

Row 23: P2, FC, P2, P2tog, K4, M1, P1, FC, P1, M1, K4, P2tog, P1, P2tog, K4, M1, P1, BC, P1, M1, K4, P2tog, P2, BC, P2.

Row 25: P2, K4, P1, P2tog, *(K4, P2) twice, K4*, P3tog, rep from * to *, end P2tog, P1, K4, P2.

Row 26: Rep row 2.

Row 27: Rep row 7.

Row 28: Rep row 2.

Rep rows 1–28.

PATTERN 2: ENSIGN'S BRAID WITH CABLES (PANEL OF 36 STS)
Make 2.

NOTES:

Front Cross (FC): Sl 2 to dpn and hold in front, K2, then K2 from dpn.

Back Cross (BC): Sl 2 to dpn and hold in back, K2, then K2 from dpn.

front cross (fc): Sl 3 to dpn and hold in front, K3, then K3 from dpn.

back cross (bc): Sl 3 to dpn and hold in back, K3, then K3 from dpn.

Single Front Cross (SFC): Sl 3 to dpn and hold in front, P1, then K3 from dpn.

Single Back Cross (SBC): Sl 1 to dpn and hold in back, K3, then P1 from dpn.

Row 1 (RS): Sl 1, P1, K4, P2, K3, P4, K6, P4, K3, P2, K4, P2.

Row 2: Sl 1, K1, P4, K2, P3, K4, P6, K4, P3, K2, P4, K2.

Row 3: Sl 1, P1, FC, P2, K3, P4, bc, P4, K3, P2, BC, P2.

Row 4 and all WS rows: Work sts as they face you (remember to sl first st in patt every row).

Row 5: Sl 1, P1, K4, P2, (SFC, P2, SBC) twice, P2, K4, P2.

Row 7: Sl 1, P1, FC, P3, SFC, SBC, P2, SFC, SBC, P3 BC, P2.

Row 9: Sl 1, P1, K4, P4, fc, P4, bc, P4, K4, P2.

Row 11: Sl 1, P1, FC, P3, SBC, SFC, P2, SBC, SFC, P3, BC, P2.

Row 13: Sl 1, P1, K4, P2, (SBC, P2, SFC) twice, P2, K4, P2.

Row 15: Sl 1, P1, FC, P2, K3, P4, fc, P4, K3, P2, BC, P2.

Row 17: Rep row 5.

Row 19: Rep row 7.

Row 21: Sl 1, P1, K4, P4, bc, P4, fc, P4, K4, P2.

Row 23: Rep row 11.

Row 25: Rep row 13.

Rep rows 2–25.

DIRECTIONS

NOTE: To create a good selvage edge on each panel for sewing together, slip first stitch of *every* row in pattern as it faces you.

1. With red yarn, CO 49 sts and work in patt 1 until work measures approximately 48". BO on row 24 of the 7th rep of the patt.
2. Make 2 more patt 1 panels in red.
3. With dark navy yarn, CO 36 sts and work in patt 2 until work measures approximately 48". BO on row 19 of the 8th rep of the patt.
4. Make 1 more patt 2 panel in dark navy.

FINISHING

1. Join the panels together, referring to "Joining Stockinette Stitch Edges" on page 90: red panels on both sides and in the center with the 2 narrower navy panels in between.
2. Overstitch 5 panels together with gold braid as shown.
3. Steam to block.
4. Referring to "Tassels" on page 91, make 4 tassels using navy yarn and gold braid and attach to 4 corners of throw with gold braid as shown at left.

PENNE WITH PROSCIUTTO AND ARUGULA

We grow arugula all summer long in our gardens and just can't ever seem to get enough of it. This is one of our favorite summer pastas. It's easy to make, takes just a few minutes to prepare, and combines some of our favorite flavors. The arugula seems almost overwhelming when first added but very quickly wilts to the perfect quantity for this refreshing warm weather pasta!

INGREDIENTS

1 pound penne pasta

¼ pound prosciutto, thinly sliced and chopped into ¼" pieces

2 tablespoons fresh lemon juice

2 tablespoons capers, drained

1 bunch fresh arugula* (approximately 1 pound), washed, stems removed, and coarsely chopped

24 Kalamata olives, pitted and halved

⅓ cup grated Parmesan Reggiano

2 tablespoons olive oil

1 tablespoon grated lemon peel

Salt and pepper to taste

DIRECTIONS

1. Cook pasta until al dente (tender but still firm to bite).
2. Meanwhile, sauté chopped prosciutto until edges are just beginning to brown. Just before pasta is finished cooking, add lemon juice and capers to prosciutto and heat through.
3. Drain penne, reserving ⅔ cup of water.
4. Toss pasta with prosciutto mixture, arugula, olives, and Parmesan Reggiano. Drizzle with olive oil and toss again with grated lemon peel. Salt and pepper to taste. Add reserved water if needed.

Or substitute fresh watercress or spinach if arugula is unavailable.

Serves 4.

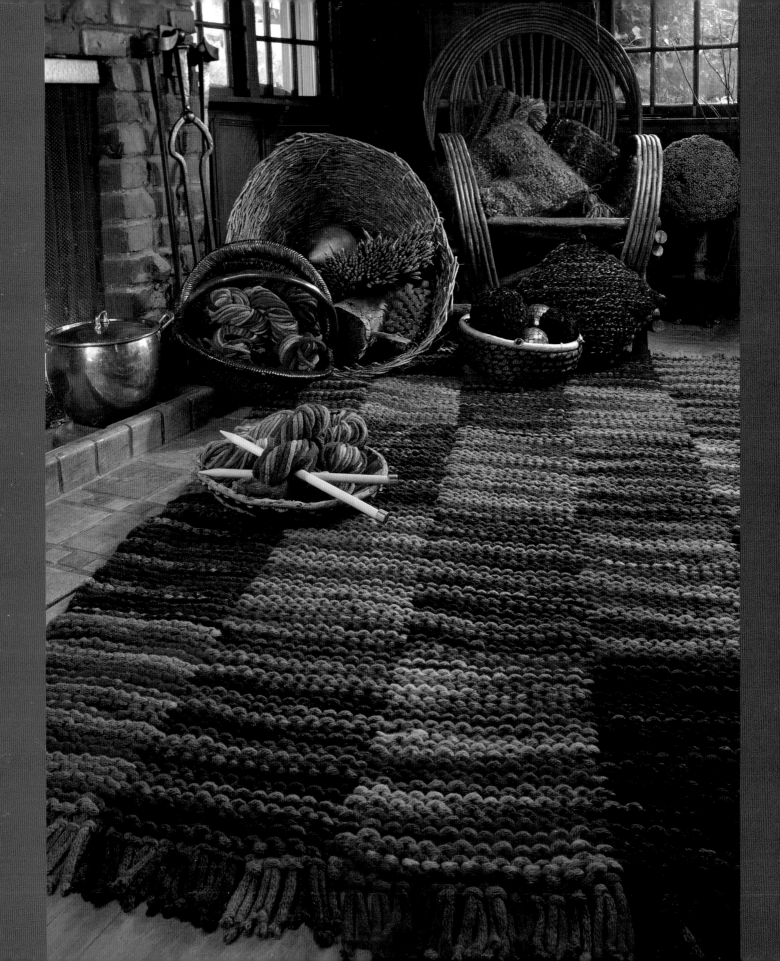

THE MAGIC CARPET

Our good friend Holly and her son are very fortunate to live overlooking Lake Washington, in one of the first homes to be built in the area. It was originally designed as a hunting lodge on what was, at the turn of the century when it was built, the "outskirts" of Seattle. Her log house with its great central fireplace provides the perfect setting for our sumptuous, richly colored rug. We were instantly fascinated with the colors and texture of this beautiful, ropy yarn and couldn't imagine a better use for it than this rug! Holly and Will spend many crisp winter nights in front of their fire. What better way to warm a winter chill than with this hearty chicken soup?

Size: 60" x 90"

MATERIALS

Use a very chunky yarn that knits at 1.2 sts to 1".
50 skeins of Noro Big Tubu (approx. 28 yds/skein)
- 10 skeins purple 45 (A)
- 12 skeins brown 47 (B)
- 8 skeins orange 75 (C)
- 12 skeins black 53 (D)
- 8 skeins pink 102 (E)

#19 needles
Large tapestry needle and upholstery-weight thread for
joining panels

GAUGE

4.8 sts and 10.6 rows = 4" in garter st
Always check gauge before starting project. Increase or
decrease needle size to obtain correct gauge.

DIRECTIONS

The rug is knit in 12" x 90" strips that are sewn together.
1. With color A, CO 14 sts and work 47 rows in garter st.
2. With color D, work 48 rows in garter st.
3. With color E, work 48 rows in garter st.
4. With color B, work 48 rows in garter st.
5. With color C, work 47 rows in garter st. BO all sts on
   48th row.
6. Make 4 more panels, substituting colors as shown.

TIP

We used all five colors because we loved them all, but for a more conservative rug, you might want to limit the number of colors. We have a customer who made a beautiful runner for her hallway using just one color.

FINISHING

1. Working from right side, join panels securely, referring to "Joining Garter Stitch Edges" on page 90 and aligning color changes from one panel to next.

2. Using individual 10" lengths of Big Tubu, color coordinated to square being fringed, place strands 1" apart along both ends of rug. See "Fringe" on page 93.

3. Knot both ends of each strand to avoid unraveling.

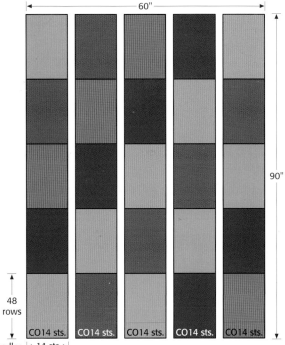

THE ULTIMATE CHICKEN SOUP

Our good friend "Chef Paul" shared this recipe with us several years ago and it has become one of our favorites. Paul's Cajun background is evident in the spices. The combination of great healthy ingredients makes this our favorite choice to take to a sick friend!

1 teaspoon whole peppercorns
1-pound package egg noodles
1 large bunch baby spinach
1 bunch scallions, chopped
1 bunch cilantro, chopped
½ bunch parsley, chopped
Salt and pepper to taste

DIRECTIONS

1. Add olive oil to Dutch oven and heat oil over medium-high heat. Add chicken and brown on both sides.
2. Remove chicken and set aside. Add garlic, shallots, celery, leeks, and carrots. Sauté until they begin to soften. Add turmeric, marjoram, oregano, and seasoning salt and continue cooking for a couple minutes more.
3. Add chicken stock. Cut chicken thighs into bite-size pieces and return to pot. Bring soup to boil.
4. Reduce heat to simmer and add peppercorns. Simmer uncovered for 45 minutes to an hour.
5. Cook egg noodles in a separate pan until al dente (tender but still firm to bite).
6. Wash and dry baby spinach.

INGREDIENTS

2 tablespoons olive oil
2½ pounds boneless, skinless chicken thighs
2 to 3 cloves garlic, peeled and chopped
6 shallots, peeled and chopped
4 center stalks celery, cut into ¼" slices
6 small to medium leeks, cut into ¼" slices
2 to 3 carrots, cut into ¼" slices
2 tablespoons ground turmeric
2 teaspoons dried marjoram
1 teaspoon dried oregano
2 teaspoons Chef Paul's Magic Seasoning Salt (or other seasoning salt)
3 quarts chicken stock

SERVING SUGGESTION

1. Place a handful of spinach leaves in bottom of each of 6 large soup bowls. Top with a sprinkling of chopped scallions, cilantro, and parsley.
2. Add a generous serving of egg noodles to each bowl.
3. Add soup to each bowl to complete. Salt and pepper to taste.

Serves 6.

PILLOW TALK

Our jewel-toned pillows are knit with the smaller companion yarn to that used for the rug on page 51. Whether tucked into her favorite willow chair or tossed on the floor by the fire for a bedtime story, these are the perfect accent in Holly's beautifully rustic log home. We introduced a silky, soft, fur-like yarn to run with the tubular "Little Tubu" for truly luxurious pillows. Our favorite recipe for oatmeal chocolate chip cookies provides the perfect accompaniment.

Sizes:

Pillow A	12" X 12"
Pillow B	16" X 16"
Pillow C	19" X 19"

MATERIALS

Use a very chunky yarn or combination of yarns that knits
at 1.7 sts to 1".

PILLOW A:

3 skeins Noro Little Tubu in black 53
(approx. 50 yds/skein)

2 skeins On Line Boom in navy multi 7
(approx. 55 yds/skein)

3 skeins Noro Little Tubu in purple 45

2 skeins On Line Boom in purple multi 1

One 14" x 14" pillow insert

PILLOW B:

3 skeins Noro Little Tubu in pink 102

2 skeins On Line Boom in lavender 2

3 skeins Noro Little Tubu in orange 75

2 skeins On Line Boom in orange 4

2 buttons, 1½" diameter

One 16" x 16" pillow insert

PILLOW C:

5 skeins Noro Little Tubu in brown 47

2 skeins S. Charles Micio in black 9
(approx. 110 yds/skein)

1 skein S. Charles Micio in brown 5

1 skein GGH Cometa, color 003, for trim only
(approx. 55 yds/skein)

One 16" x 16" pillow insert

#19 needles for all pillows

GAUGE

6.8 sts and 12 rows = 4" in garter st

Always check gauge before starting project. Increase or
decrease needle size to obtain correct gauge.

DIRECTIONS
PILLOW A

▶ **Back**

1. With Little Tubu 53 and Boom 7 held together as one,
CO 2 sts and inc 1 st at beg of *every* row by knitting into
front and back of first st. Cont in garter st, inc until you
have 30 sts on needles.

2. Dec 1 st at beg of every row by sl 1, K1, PSSO until you
are back to 2 sts on your needles. Your work should be
a square.

3. BO last 2 sts.

▶ **Front**

With Little Tubu 45 and Boom 1 held together as one, CO
2 sts and work as for back.

▶ **Finishing**

1. Sew 3 sides of the front and back of the pillow together.
Insert 14" pillow form and sew opening closed.

2. Using 5 yards each of both colors of Little Tubu and
navy multi Boom, make a twisted cord referring to
"Twisted Cords" on page 92.

3. Wrap the perimeter of the pillow as shown with the
completed cord, knotting twice at each of the 4 corners;
blindstitch in place.

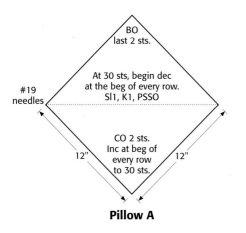

Pillow A

(Diagram labels:)
BO last 2 sts.

At 30 sts, begin dec at the beg of every row. Sl1, K1, PSSO

#19 needles

CO 2 sts. Inc at beg of every row to 30 sts.

12"   12"

4. Place 1 button in the center of each side of the pillow and sew in place firmly, pulling thread tight so that buttons pull in the center of the pillow.

PILLOW B

◗ Front

1. With Little Tubu 75 and Boom 4 held together as one, CO 29 sts.

   Row 1 (RS): K1, *K3, P3*, rep from * to *, end K1.

   Rows 2, 4, 6, 8, 10, and 12: Knit edge sts, then work all other sts as they face you.

   Row 3: K1, P1, *K3, P3*, rep from * to *, end K1.

   Row 5: K1, P2, *K3, P3*, rep from * to *, end K1.

   Row 7: K1, P3, *K3, P3*, rep from * to *, end K1.

   Row 9: K1, K1, P3, *K3, P3*, rep from * to *, end K1.

   Row 11: K1, K2, P3, *K3, P3*, rep from * to *, end K1.

   Rep rows 1–12.

   NOTE: Because you are moving the pattern 1 stitch to the right on every right-side row, you will not end every row with a complete pattern repeat.

2. Cont in 12-row patt until work measures 16" from beg. BO all sts.

◗ Back

With Little Tubu 102 and Boom 2 held together as one, CO 29 sts and work as for front.

◗ Finishing

1. Sew 3 sides of the front and back of the pillow together. Insert 16" pillow form and sew opening closed.

2. Referring to "Tassels" on page 91, make 4 tassels with 2 strands each of Little Tubu and Boom colors (total 8 strands). Wrap a 4" square of cardboard 8 times. Wrap the neck of each of the tassels with a strand of each color of Boom 6 times and secure ends.

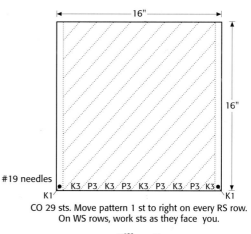

(Diagram labels:)
16"

16"

#19 needles

K1   K3 P3 K3 P3 K3 P3 K3 P3 K3   K1

CO 29 sts. Move pattern 1 st to right on every RS row. On WS rows, work sts as they face you.

Pillow B

3. Referring to "Twisted Cords" on page 92, make 4 twisted cords to secure the tassels; use two 80" strands of each of the 2 Little Tubu colors.

Cut.

PILLOW C

Patt st is an uneven multiple of 3.

▶ Back

1. With Little Tubu 47 and Micio 5 held together as one, CO 27 sts. Work every row: (K2, P1) across row to last 3 sts, end K3.

2. Cont in patt until work measures 15" from beg. BO all sts.

▶ Front

1. With Little Tubu 47 and Micio 9 held together as one, CO 37 sts.

   Rows 1–6: Knit (garter st).

   Rows 7–51: K5, (K2, P1) across row to last 5 sts, end K5.

   Rows 52–55: Knit (garter st).

2. BO all sts on 56th row.

▶ Finishing

1. Center smaller pillow back on pillow front, inside garter border. Stitch together to create a flanged border. Insert 16" pillow form and sew opening closed.

2. Referring to "Twisted Cords" on page 92, make 2 twisted cords, each approximately 65" long, each made from 4 strands of 4½ yards of Little Tubu 47.

3. Wrap 1 strand of the bronze Cometa metallic yarn around completed twisted cord as shown.

4. Sew a twisted cord on front and back of pillow where flange meets pillow.

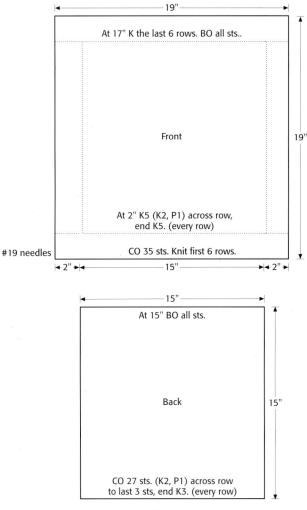

Pillow C

AMAZING OATMEAL AND CHOCOLATE CHIP COOKIES

Everyone has a favorite recipe for chocolate chip cookies—ours is a compilation of what we like best from a number of recipes and our own trial and error over years of cookie baking. We both love the crunchy texture of the oatmeal with the richness of the chocolate chips and the unexpected sweetness of the raisins.

½ teaspoon salt

1 teaspoon cinnamon

⅛ teaspoon nutmeg

2¾ cups uncooked oats

½ cup golden raisins

1½ cups real chocolate chips

DIRECTIONS

1. Preheat oven to 350°.
2. In a large frying pan over medium-low heat, toast the pecans and wheat germ for 10 to 15 minutes, stirring frequently to avoid burning. Remove from pan and set aside.
3. Cream butter, brown sugar, and white sugar together until fluffy.
4. Beat in egg and vanilla.
5. Add flour, baking soda, salt, cinnamon, and nutmeg; mix well.
6. Add uncooked oats, pecan and wheat germ mixture, raisins, and chocolate chips; mix well.
7. Drop rounded soup-spoonfuls onto ungreased cookie sheet.
8. Bake for 15 to 18 minutes or until golden brown.

Yield: approximately 45 cookies

INGREDIENTS

¾ cup pecans, chopped

½ cup wheat germ

½ pound plus 4 tablespoons (2½ sticks) butter

½ cup brown sugar

½ cup white sugar

1 egg

1 teaspoon vanilla

1½ cups unsifted flour

1 teaspoon baking soda

FRINGED FANTASY

Laura is a long-time true friend of ours. We remain in awe of her ability to find time to knit daily, entertain frequently, train for and run at least one marathon a year (and sometimes more), support the events of the four different schools that her sons attend, and somehow manage never to forget a carpool rotation or miss a single game for any of her children! Her beautiful home is filled with knitting projects she has made. We particularly loved the way the warm, rich colors and cozy softness of this throw provided the perfect accent to the room. Laura is a great cook in addition to her other numerous attributes; this healthy, delicious salad is one of her hallmarks.

Size: 48" x 60"

MATERIALS

Use a very chunky yarn or combination of smaller yarns that knits at 2.2 sts to 1".

11 skeins Euro Yarns Brushstrokes Mohair (approx. 110 yds/skein)

Approximately 2400 to 3000 yds of a combination of yarns that will be used along with the mohair to keep the gauge relatively consistent as you knit

#17 circular needles (47")

Size J crochet hook

GAUGE

8.8 sts and 12 rows = 4" in St st

Always check gauge before starting project. Increase or decrease needle size to obtain correct gauge.

DIRECTIONS

1. With mohair plus 1 to 3 additional strands of yarn (based on size), CO 132 sts and K every row.
2. At end of every 2 to 3 rows, cut your yarns—except the continuous mohair blender—and leave tails about 6" to 8" long. (These will become fringe at ends of throw.)

NOTE: The mohair base yarn will run through the entire throw for consistency and blending, but you can change the other combinations every 3 or more rows as you knit. Remember that all yarns do not need to change at the same time; some may only appear once and others may be re-introduced a number of times throughout the throw. To vary the look of the throw, you may also want to use the same yarns but in different combinations. The idea is to keep the gauge of the combinations of yarns fairly consistent as you knit. Do remember that this is an art, not a science, so your gauge may not be exactly the same in every row—but it should be similar.

3. Cont in garter st, changing yarns and remembering to cut tails at end of every 3 or 4 rows until your work measures 48" when laid flat.
4. BO all sts.

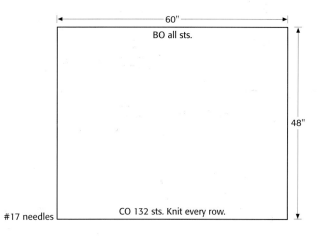

FINISHING

Add additional yarn fringe across both ends of throw as follows:

- With leftover yarn, make groups of yarns, about 12" long with 12 to 14 strands each. Referring to "Fringe" on page 93 and using a large crochet hook, add a group of yarn at every other rib across both ends.
- Knot each group evenly across both ends of throw, as shown in photo below.
- Divide each group in half and connect each half with the half from the adjacent group.
- Trim all ends even.

WILD GREENS WITH ROASTED ASPARAGUS, NEW POTATOES, AND CHICKEN

This is another of our favorite "one-dish meals." We've listed the ingredients we most frequently use, but the truth
is that we very often go through the refrigerator and add whatever we find that needs to be eaten!
Can anyone ever really get enough of a great salad?

INGREDIENTS

6 to 8 cups mixed baby salad greens, preferably organic

2 cups warm, shredded, roasted chicken (we purchase hot
    roasted chickens at our local deli)

3 to 4 paper-thin slices of red onion, separated

¼ yellow or orange bell pepper, seeded and chopped

1 tomato, seeded and chopped

¼ cup fresh cilantro, chopped (or substitute parsley)

⅓ cup Parmesan Reggiano, freshly grated

1 tablespoon Balsamic vinegar

2 teaspoons white wine or tarragon vinegar

4 tablespoons roasted garlic–flavored olive oil

1 to 2 tablespoons fresh lemon juice

Salt and pepper to taste

2 to 3 cloves garlic, peeled and thinly sliced

10 to 12 small new red potatoes (approximately 1½" in
    diameter), halved

1 bunch asparagus, cleaned and cut into 1½" pieces

⅓ cup pine nuts, toasted

DIRECTIONS

1. Preheat oven to 450°.
2. Wash and dry greens thoroughly (we love salad spinners!), place in a large linen towel, and put in refrigerator.
3. Bone and shred roasted chicken, cover to keep warm, and set aside.
4. In the bottom of a large salad bowl, combine onion, bell pepper, tomato, cilantro, and half of the Parmesan Reggiano.
5. Add vinegars and 2 tablespoons of olive oil and toss to mix well. Add lemon juice and salt and pepper to taste. Set aside, tossing occasionally and keeping at room temperature.
6. Place remaining olive oil and sliced garlic in the bottom of a shallow roasting pan and heat through until oil begins to sizzle.
7. Add potatoes to roasting pan and return to hot oven. Roast for about 20 minutes, stirring occasionally to prevent sticking.
8. Add asparagus and return to hot oven for another 10 to 12 minutes, tossing frequently. Remove when potatoes are tender and asparagus is beginning to brown.
9. Add chicken, pine nuts, and wild greens to salad bowl and toss to coat.
10. Add roasted vegetables (including the crispy brown bits of garlic) and toss again. Top with the rest of the Parmesan Reggiano and serve with a great crusty bread.

Serves 4 as a main course.

NOTE: We like our salads lightly dressed and enjoy the flavor of the oil from the roasted vegetables as well. If you like your salads more heavily dressed, you may want to increase the amounts of oil and vinegar.

STADIUM BLANKET

Our photographer, Brent Kane, described this shot as "The way we all wish our college dorms had looked!" As with Fringed Fantasy, we photographed this blanket in Laura's home; we know that her four boys—all athletes—make their home feel pretty close to a dorm at times. We used the University of Washington as the inspiration for our stadium blanket, but we have provided the tools needed to personalize this throw for any school you might prefer. Our easy and truly delicious recipe for spicy sweet-hot popcorn that is prepared in a micro-wave (perfect for dorm life) seemed an obvious accompaniment.

Size: 48" x 48"

GAUGE

10 sts and 12 rows = 4" in St st

Always check gauge before starting project. Increase or decrease needle size to obtain correct gauge.

DOUBLE SEED STITCH PATTERN

Row 1: K1, P1 across row.

Row 2: P1, K1 across row.

Row 3: Rep row 1.

Row 4: Rep row 2.

Row 5: P1, K1 across row.

Row 6: K1, P1 across row.

Row 7: Rep row 5.

Row 8: Rep row 6.

Rep rows 1–8.

DIRECTIONS
LETTER SQUARES

1. With Baby, CO 58 sts and work 9 rows in garter st.
2. Work the next 18" in double seed st patt as follows:.
   Row 1 (RS): K7, *K1, P1*, rep from * to *, end K7.
   Row 2 (WS): K7, *P1, K1*, rep from * to *, end K7.
   Row 3: Rep row 1.
   Row 4: Rep row 2.
   Row 5: K7, *P1, K1*, rep from * to *, end K7.
   Row 6: K7, K1, P1*, rep from * to *, end K7.
   Row 7: Rep row 5.
   Row 8: Rep row 6.
   Rep these 8 rows until work measures 21" from beg.
3. Work 9 rows garter st and BO on 10th row.
4. Make a second square exactly as the first.

STRIPED SQUARES

1. With Baby, CO 58 sts and work 9 rows in garter st.
2. Work the next 18 rows in striping patt as follows:
   Beg and end each row with 7 sts of garter st using Baby.

MATERIALS

Use a yarn that knits at 2.5 sts to 1".

12 skeins Tahki Yarns Baby (approx. 60 yds/skein)

7 skeins GGH Gala (approx. 93 yds/skein)

6 skeins Horst Mulberseide Schurwolle (approx. 110 yds/skein)

#17 needles

Large tapestry needle

The center 44 sts should be striped in St st as follows:
- 8 rows Gala and Mulberseide Schurwolle held together.
- 8 rows Baby
- Rep 3 more times, end with 8 rows Gala and Mulberseide Schurwolle held together.

3. With Baby, work 9 rows in garter st and BO on tenth row.

4. Make a second square exactly as the first.

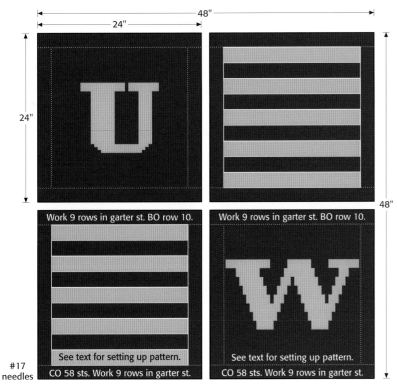

Striped Square

Letter Square

FINISHING

1. Using the appropriate letters for the school or university you have selected (see alphabet chart on pages 71–72), duplicate stitch a letter in the center of each of the solid-color squares, referring to "Duplicate Stitch" at right and on page 70.

2. Join the 4 squares as shown in the diagram at left, referring to "Joining Garter Stitch Edges" on page 00.

3. Make 4 tassels with Baby, wrapped with the Gala and Mulberseide Schurwolle combination. Make twisted cords with all 3 yarns to attach tassels to throw. See "Tassels" and "Twisted Cords" on pages 91–92.

DUPLICATE STITCH

To do horizontal duplicate stitching, thread a tapestry needle with the desired color of yarn. Bring the needle from back to front at base of knit stitch you wish to cover with a duplicate stitch. Working from right to left, insert needle under base of knitted stitch directly above stitch you wish to cover.

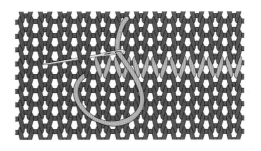

Bring needle down and insert it at base of the same knit stitch. Bring tip of needle out at base of next stitch you wish to cover. Repeat this process until you have covered all the horizontal stitches indicated in the design. Weave in ends on wrong side.

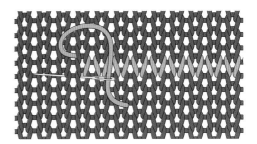

To do vertical duplicate stitching, bring a threaded tapestry needle from back to front, at base of first stitch to be covered. Working from bottom up, insert needle from right to left through the top of same stitch. Bring needle down and insert it at base of same stitch, bringing it out again at base of stitch that lies directly above the one you just covered. Continue in this manner until you reach the final vertical duplicate stitch; then pull yarn through to wrong side and weave in ends.

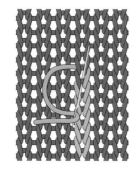

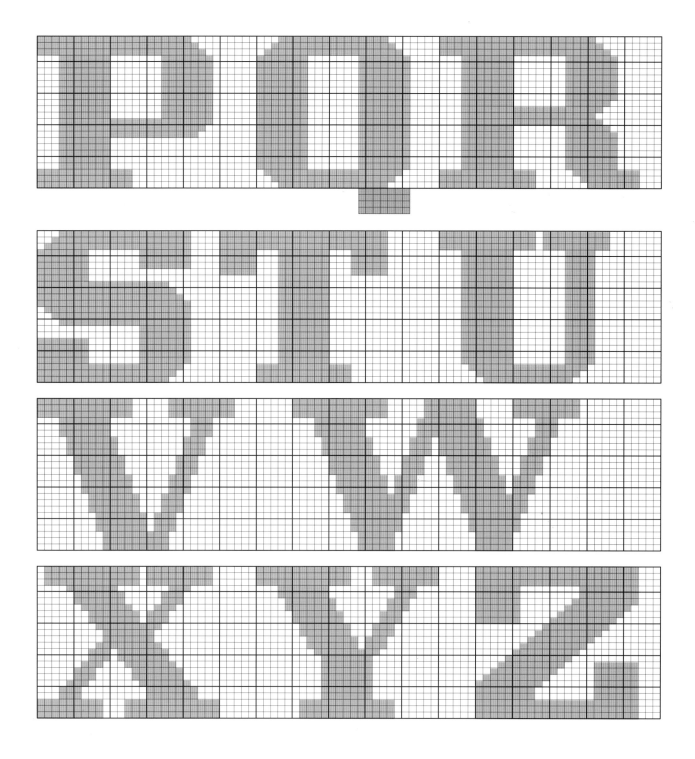

GOURMET POPCORN

Popcorn is one of those foods that almost everyone loves! This is our own microwave version—perfect for dorm living!

This is a recipe that really tastes much more complex than it is to make.

INGREDIENTS

1½ teaspoons cumin

½ cup plus 1 tablespoon granulated sugar

½ teaspoon red pepper flakes

¼ cup water

1 package microwave popcorn (plain, unflavored)

2 tablespoons salted butter, melted

Salt to taste

DIRECTIONS

1. Mix together cumin, 1 tablespoon sugar, and red pepper flakes and set aside.

2. Place ½ cup sugar and water in a Pyrex measuring cup and cover with plastic wrap. Microwave for 4½ minutes on high, checking at 10-second intervals. Remove from microwave when mixture has turned very pale amber, but do not disturb plastic wrap. Set aside. The mixture will darken naturally as it sits.

3. Microwave popcorn according to package directions.

4. In a large bowl, drizzle popcorn with melted butter and spice mixture. Add salt if desired.

5. Prick plastic wrap with a fork to release steam. (Caution: very hot!) Remove plastic wrap and pour mixture over popcorn, stirring to coat as many kernels as possible. Popcorn will crisp as it cools.

COLORFUL KIDS

Our friend Beverly is one of the most colorful kids around! At ten, Beverly is a uniquely imaginative writer, never far from her laptop; an accomplished pianist unafraid to accompany a roomful of adults singing carols; and a fierce competitor on the soccer field. Beverly is a ballerina with surprising grace and beautiful natural form; a talented artist whose caricatures are instantly recognizable; and a sly, sneaky practical joker with a somewhat wicked sense of humor. Our throw works perfectly in her cheerful, cozy room. A sign on the door clearly states, "Welcome everyone but enemies." I guess we passed the test, as we were allowed in to photograph. Beverly personally decorated the shortbread cookies, favorites of hers (with a little help from her mom).

Size: 46" x 46"

MATERIALS

Use a very chunky yarn or combination of yarns that knits at 2.5 sts to 1".

31 skeins Lang Nuvola (approx. 27 yds/skein)

1 skein each of:
- white 0002
- lavender 0046
- celery 0097

2 skeins each of:
- navy 0035
- burgundy 0062
- purple 0090
- olive 0099
- teal 0088

3 skeins each of:
- fuchsia 0085
- red 0060
- yellow 0013
- orange 0059
- berry 0061
- denim 0021

#13 circular needles (47")

Approximately 50 colorful, washable, flat buttons in a variety of shapes and colors
- 16 buttons, 1½" diameter
- 24 buttons, ¾" diameter

Large tapestry needle

STRIPING PATTERN

Color 1	burgundy	3½ rows
Color 2	white	1½ rows
Color 3	purple	3½ rows
Color 4	denim	4½ rows
Color 5	yellow	4½ rows
Color 6	lavender	1½ rows

Color 7	red	4½ rows
Color 8	olive	3½ rows
Color 9	fuschia	4½ rows
Color 10	orange	4½ rows
Color 11	navy	3½ rows
Color 12	teal	3½ rows
Color 13	berry	4½ rows
Color 14	celery	1½ rows

GAUGE

10 sts and 11 rows = 4" in St st

Always check gauge before starting project. Increase or decrease needle size to obtain correct gauge.

DIRECTIONS

1. CO 110 sts and work 3" in garter st, following striping patt. When you change colors, do so randomly in the middle of a row, and at each color transition K both old and new colors together for 6 sts. As you change colors, leave a 3" tail of new yarn you are adding at the back of your work. As you transition to next color, leave a 3" tail of yarn you are finishing at front of your work. While transitions from one color to next are random, space them across row so that they do not line up as you progress.

2. When work measures 3" from beg, switch to St st for body of throw but K first and last 7 sts on every row to create a garter-st border.

3. Cont to follow color striping patt until work measures 43" from beg. Switch to garter st and cont (following the striping patt) until work measures 46" from beg. BO all sts.

NOTE: When you change colors in the stockinette portion of the throw, always purl the 6 stitches of the combined yarns on the knit side of your work, or knit the 6 stitches if the transition occurs on the purl side of the work. See "Tip" on page 78.

FINISHING

CAUTION: Do not add buttons if this throw is intended for a small child.

1. Working on RS of throw, place large and small buttons randomly across throw where loose ends from changing colors occur. Split ends of yarn, and with a large tapestry needle, thread half of strand through one hole of button from back to front and thread other half of strand in same manner through another hole in same button. Tie 4 overhand knots to secure button and trim ends to 1". Fluff ends to make them fuzzy.

2. Working on WS of throw, split all ends left loose on this side. Tie 4 overhand knots using 2 halves of each strand, trim ends to 1" and fluff as on front. Hint: Use the point of tapestry needle and run it through 1" ends of knotted yarns until they are fuzzy.

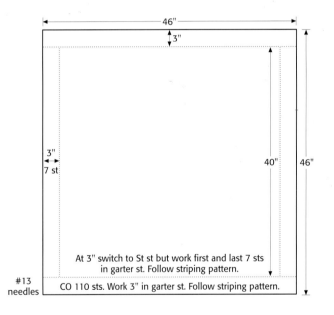

3. Make 4 tassels using remaining yarn from throw, but instead of finishing tassel as you would a traditional tassel, take loose strips of cut fibers, using 1 strand to tie them in the center to create a "bundle." Now, using your tapestry needle, attach one of the "bundles" to each corner of throw as shown to create a free-form tassel.

TIP

Read your pattern from beginning to end before you start knitting. Our knitter (an experienced, detail-oriented person) somehow didn't realize that the directions said to P6 sts on the K side and K6 sts on the P side each time colors were changed. The good news is that all mistakes aren't a tragedy. We loved the throw as it was knit and decided to show it here.

SHORTBREAD HEARTS

This is a recipe adapted from one by my childhood best friend's Swedish grandmother. One of my earliest memories is of sitting in her kitchen with warm shortbread and a cold glass of milk. Is there anything better? —Lindy

INGREDIENTS

¾ cup granulated sugar
1½ cups butter, at room temperature
4 cups white flour

DIRECTIONS

1. Preheat oven to 325°.
2. Cream sugar and butter together thoroughly.
3. Add flour one cup at a time, mixing well.
4. Roll dough onto lightly floured surface and cut cookies with a heart-shaped cookie cutter.
5. Bake for 34 to 39 minutes.

Yield: approximately 2 dozen cookies

VELVET TOUCH

What a gentle way to start a life! Nestled in an incredibly plush, velvety blanket, surrounded by soft light and hazy pastels, tucked in at the foot of Mom and Dad's bed. Could there possibly be a more secure, serene nest than this? Our customers fall in love with the velvety texture of this yarn. That it is machine washable makes this throw the perfect new baby gift. Our friend Elizabeth developed the recipe for these healthy, natural gelatin hearts that every child finds irresistible!

Size: 34" x 34"

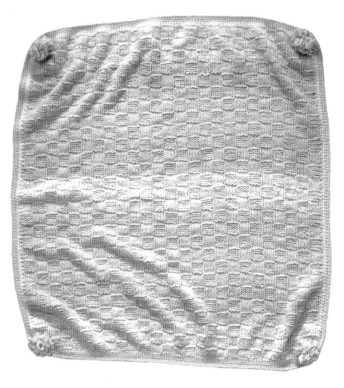

MATERIALS

Use a yarn that knits at 3 sts to 1".

13 skeins Lang Velvet Touch (approx. 115 yds/skein)

    5 skeins variegated 1210 (A)

    2 skeins white 1200 (B)

    2 skeins green 1207 (C)

    2 skeins yellow 1206 (D)

    2 skeins blue 1208 (E)

#10¾ needles

Size I crochet hook

GAUGE

12 sts and 16 rows = 4" in patt

Always check gauge before starting project. Increase or decrease needle size to obtain correct gauge.

DIRECTIONS

1. With colors A and B held together as one, CO 102 sts and work as follows:

   Rows 1, 3, 5 (RS): K1, (K4, P4) across row, end K4, K1.

   Row 2 and all even-numbered rows in colors as stated: Work sts as they face you.

   Rows 7, 9, 11: K1, (P4, K4) across row, end P4, K1.

   Rows 13, 15, 17: Rep rows 1–6.

   Rows 18: Work sts as they face you.

2. With colors A and C, work RS rows as follows and on WS rows work sts as they face you:

   Rows 19, 21, 23 (RS): K1, (P4, K4) across row, end P4, K1.

   Rows 25, 27, 29: K1, (K4, P4) across row, end K4, K1.

   Rows 31, 33, 35: Rep rows 19–24.

   Rows 36: Work sts as they face you.

3. With colors A and D, work rows 37–54 as rows 1–18.

4. With colors A and E, work rows 55–72 as rows 19–36.

5. With colors A and B, work rows 73–90 as rows 1–18.

6. With colors A and C, work rows 91–108 as rows 19–36.

7. With colors A and D, work rows 109–126 as rows 1–18.

TIP

With chenille yarns, we prefer to use metal "turbo" circular needles. We find that they allow the chenille to move smoothly and avoid the tendency to stick to the needles.

8. With colors A and E, work rows 127–144 as rows 19–36.

9. With colors A and B, work final rows 145–162 as rows 1–18.

10. BO all sts on next row.

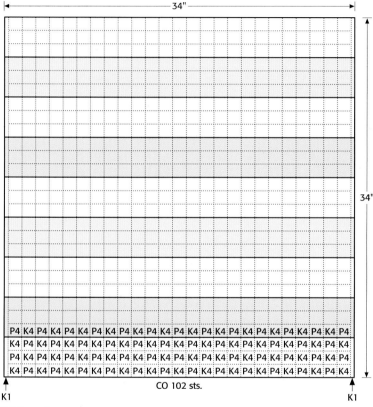

34"

34"

P4 K4 P4 K4 P4 K4 P4 K4 P4 K4 P4 K4 P4 K4 P4 K4 P4 K4 P4 K4 P4 K4 P4 K4 P4 K4 P4
K4 P4 K4 P4 K4 P4 K4 P4 K4 P4 K4 P4 K4 P4 K4 P4 K4 P4 K4 P4 K4 P4 K4 P4 K4 P4 K4
P4 K4 P4 K4 P4 K4 P4 K4 P4 K4 P4 K4 P4 K4 P4 K4 P4 K4 P4 K4 P4 K4 P4 K4 P4 K4 P4
K4 P4 K4 P4 K4 P4 K4 P4 K4 P4 K4 P4 K4 P4 K4 P4 K4 P4 K4 P4 K4 P4 K4 P4 K4 P4 K4

CO 102 sts.

K1   K1

#10¾ needles

FINISHING

1. With color A, work 2 rows of sc around 4 sides of throw.

2. Follow this with 1 row each of sc using E, then D, and finally C.

3. With equal quantities of all of your remaining yarns, make 4 small tassels for corners of throw. Make twisted cords, each approximately 15" to 20" long. Attach tassels with twisted cord tied into bows. Sew in place so that bows cannot come untied. See "Tassels" and "Twisted Cords" on pages 91–92.

NOTE: To make the small-sized tassel for this throw, use a 3" cardboard template and complete 12 wraps using all colors of Velvet Touch.

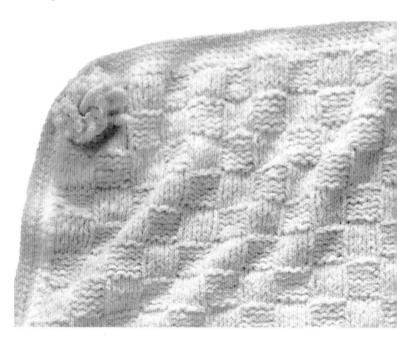

GELATIN FRUIT HEARTS

Every mom wants only healthy food for her baby. Elizabeth, our friend and Tricoter staffer, is not only a great mom but a terrific cook as well. This is her recipe for very special homemade gelatin fruit hearts that she makes with her daughter Beverly.

12 teaspoons (or 6 packages) of plain gelatin
Flavorless cooking spray
A combination of any of the following fruits:
    sliced banana
    grapes, seeded and halved
    raspberries
    blueberries
    strawberries, stems removed and berries halved
    (Avoid acidic fruits such as kiwi, orange, or grapefruit;
    they will not allow the gelatin to set properly.)
12-cup heart-shaped muffin pan

DIRECTIONS

1. Chill 3 cups of juice and completely dissolve gelatin in chilled juice.
2. Coat inside of each muffin cup with cooking spray.
3. Pour ¼ cup of juice and gelatin mixture into each of the muffin cups.
4. Heat remaining 3 cups of juice until just below boiling. Add ¼ cup heated juice to each of the muffin cups and refrigerate for about ½ hour (until just cool and beginning to set).
5. Add 2 to 5 pieces of fruit to each muffin cup (depending on size of slices or berries)
6. Refrigerate for 3 to 4 hours or until completely set.
7. Remove from tins and serve chilled.

Serves 6.

INGREDIENTS

6 cups clear fruit juice (such as apple, cranberry, or white or purple grape)

NOTE: You may use a variety of juices, mixing 1 cup juice with 2 teaspoons gelatin, to create fun colors. We made 1 cup of each color.

SOME KNITTING BASICS

here are a few knitting basics that may be second nature to many knitters, but we have found they can never be repeated too many times. Here is our list of basics.

CASTING ON

Cast on to a needle one size larger than the one specified; then change to the specified needle size on your first row. This ensures that your cast-on row is not too tight.

KNITTING YOUR EDGE STITCHES

We always knit the first and last stitch of every row (including purl and patt rows). This creates a clean, uniform "selvage edge" for weaving pieces together. These edge stitches are included in our patterns.

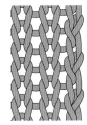

Selvage edge of
stockinette stitch

PICKING UP DROPPED STITCHES

It is not unusual to drop a stitch and for that stitch to unravel down one or more rows. Use a crochet hook to pick up the dropped stitches. If you drop a stitch on a knit row, insert the hook, front to back, into the loop of the dropped stitch. Use the hook to catch the first horizontal "ladder" in the knitting and pull it through the loop to the front. Continue in this manner through all the ladders. Place the loop on the needle, making certain that the right side of the U is on the front of the needle.

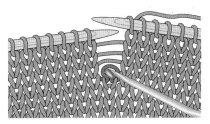

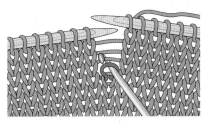

Picking up a dropped knit stitch

If you drop a stitch on a purl row, turn the work around and correct as described above for the knit side, making sure to turn the work back around to finish the purl row. Or, you can pick up the dropped stitch from behind by inserting the crochet hook, back to front, into the loop of the dropped stitch, placing the first horizontal ladder in front of the stitch, and pulling the ladder through the loop to the back. Continue in this manner through all the ladders. Place the last loop on the needle, making sure the right side of the U is on the front of the needle.

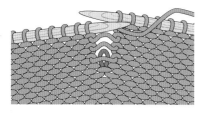

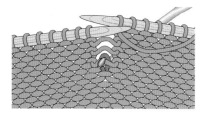

Picking up a dropped purl stitch

When an edge stitch drops and unravels, there will be no visible ladders to chain up with a crochet hook. Instead, you will see a large loop extending from the edge above a small loop, below which the knitted edge is intact. To correct this error, insert the crochet hook into the small loop. Holding the large loop with some tension, pull the lower portion of the large loop through the loop on the hook to form a stitch; then pull the upper part of the large loop

through the loop on the hook to form a stitch. Finally, catch the working yarn and pull it through the loop on the hook. Place the last stitch on the needle.

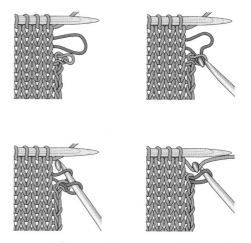

Picking up a dropped edge stitch

JOINING YARNS

There are several methods of joining yarns when starting a new skein or changing colors. We like to knit both the old and new yarn into the first stitch as you begin a row; then, dropping the old yarn, continue across the row. When you work back across the row, remember that the first stitch is just one stitch, even though you have two strands in the stitch.

Start a new skein of yarn at the beginning of a row whenever possible. When changing in the middle of a row cannot be avoided, *do not* knot the yarn. Leave a generous 3" tail from both the old and new skeins and continue knitting. These ends can be woven in securely and invisibly; knotting your yarns will leave a "scar" in your work.

WEAVING IN ENDS AS YOU KNIT

To avoid hours of laborious darning after your project is complete (particularly on projects where you change yarns frequently, or in two-color work), you should get into the practice of weaving in the ends as you go.

It is important that the weaving is done at a relaxed, even tension, or the knitting will pucker. To do this, leave ends approximately 3" on the old and new yarns; work the next two stitches with the new yarn; then, holding both yarns in your left hand, lay them over the working yarn and work the next stitch. Continue in this way, laying the ends over the working yarn on every other stitch and knitting past the ends on the following stitch for at least 2".

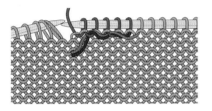

INCREASING YOUR STITCHES

There is more than one way to increase the number of stitches on your needle. You can make two stitches out of one by knitting into the front and back of the same stitch. This may also be done purlwise, by purling into the front and back of the same stitch, or it may be worked by knit one, purl one into one stitch, or by purl one, knit one into one stitch.

Another method, called "make one (M1)," adds a new stitch without leaving a hole. Insert the left-hand needle from front to back into the horizontal strand between the last stitch worked and the next stitch on the left-hand needle. Knit this strand through the back loop to twist the stitch.

DECREASING YOUR STITCHES

There are also several ways to decrease the number of stitches on your needle. With the yarn in back, slip one stitch, knit one stitch, and pass the slipped stitch over; that is, insert the point of the left-hand needle into the slipped stitch and draw it over the knit stitch and off the right-hand needle.

You can also slip the first and second stitches knitwise, one at a time, and then insert the tip of the left-hand needle into the fronts of these two stitches from the left, and knit them together from this position. This is known as slip, slip, knit (SSK).

KNITTING BASIC CABLES

For a front cross, leave the cable needle holding the stitch(es) in front of the work while working the other stitches behind it.

For a back cross, leave the cable needle holding the stitch(es) in back of the work while working the other stitches in front.

For a twisted rib, knit the second stitch first in back of the work without taking it off the needle; then knit the first stitch as usual. Take both stitches off the left-hand needle.

CROCHETED EDGES

Crocheted edges are usually narrower than knitted borders and provide a simple, clean edge. Single crochet and reverse crochet (also called crab stitch) are the most popular crocheted edges. Single crochet makes a smooth finish; crab stitch makes a decorative, bead-like finish.

SINGLE CROCHET

Working from right to left, insert the crochet hook into the knit edge stitch, draw up a loop, bring the yarn over the hook, and draw this loop through the first one. *Insert the hook into the next stitch, draw up the loop, bring the yarn over the hook again, and draw this loop through both loops on the hook*; repeat from * to * until the entire edge has been covered. Cut the yarn and secure the last loop by pulling the tail through it.

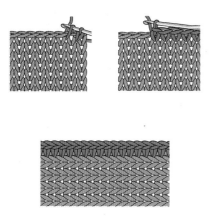

REVERSE CROCHET (CRAB STITCH)

We always work one row of single crochet first, and then follow with a row of crab stitch. Working from left to right, insert the crochet hook into a single crochet stitch, draw up a loop, bring the yarn over the hook, and draw this loop through the first one. *Insert the hook into the next stitch to the right, draw up a loop, bring the yarn over the hook again, and draw this loop through both loops on the hook*; repeat from * to * until the entire edge has been covered. Cut the yarn and secure the last loop by pulling the tail through it.

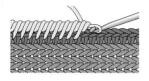

JOINING CROCHETED EDGES

Join crocheted edges with a slip stitch. Place pieces to be joined right sides together with edges aligned. Place a slip-knot on your crochet hook. Working between the first and the second stitch from the right-hand edge, insert the hook from front to back through both layers of knitting. Yarn over and pull the loop through both layers and the stitch that is on the hook. Repeat this stitch along the edge, keeping your stitches loose enough to prevent the fabric from drawing up.

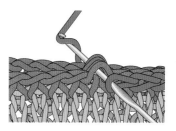

JOINING STOCKINETTE STITCH EDGES

Work this seam from the right side of the knitting, placing the pieces to be joined right side up. Begin at the lower edge and work upward, row by row. Insert a threaded tapestry needle under two horizontal bars between the first and second stitches from the edge on one side of the seam, and then under two corresponding bars on the opposite side. Continue taking stitches alternately from side to side. Pull the yarn in the direction of the seam, not toward your body, to prevent the bars from stretching to the front.

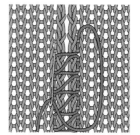

JOINING GARTER STITCH EDGES

Work this seam from the right side, placing the pieces to be joined right side up with edges aligned. With threaded tapestry needle, beginning at the lower edge of the right-hand piece, work into the top loop of the knot, and then work into the bottom loop of the corresponding knot on the left-hand side. Continue until the seam is completed.

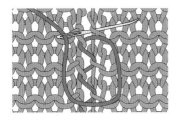

BINDING OFF

Binding off secures the last row of knitting so that it will not unravel. Binding off is also used for shaping when two or more stitches need to be eliminated at one time.

Always bind off in pattern. Many knitters tend to bind off too tightly, causing puckers and undue stress on the bound-off edge. You can prevent this problem by binding off with a knitting needle one or two sizes larger than the one called for in the pattern.

To bind off on a knit row, first knit two stitches; then, *with the two stitches on the right-hand needle, pass the right stitch over the left stitch and off the end of the needle. Knit the next stitch.* Repeat from * to * until the required number of stitches are bound off.

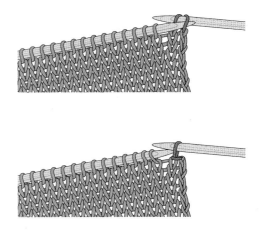

The process is the same for binding off on the purl side, except that you purl instead of knit. For ribbing, or for any other pattern stitch, bind off in the pattern; that is, knit the knit stitches and purl the purl stitches, always passing the right stitch over the left stitch and off the end of the needle. If you bind off all the stitches on the needle, cut the working yarn and pull the cut end through the last stitch to secure it.

FINISHING

BLOCKING

Blocking is the process of dampening or steaming the knitted pieces to even out the lines of the stitches and the yarn fibers. For best results, block the pieces before you sew them together. The labels on most knitting fibers give instructions for blocking. Read the instructions before you begin.

Blocking requires a flat surface larger than the knitted piece. Block on an out-of-the-way place on the carpet or make a special padded "steaming table" for this purpose. Use long, straight pins, such as quilting or stainless T-pins, to pin the pieces to the blocking surface. First pin the length of the piece and then the width, measuring carefully to ensure that it matches the dimensions given in the pattern. Place pins every 1" to prevent the piece from shrinking as it dries. If you block on a very large surface, such as a carpet, you may pin the pieces next to each other, lining up the selvage edges that will be steamed to make sure the seams are even.

Hold a steamer or iron set on the steam setting ½" above the knitted surface and direct the steam over the entire surface, except the ribbing. There are several good hand steamers on the market today in the $40 to $50 range. You can get similar results by placing wet cheesecloth on top of the knitted surface and touching it lightly with a dry iron. Do not press down or use a forward or sideways motion.

If your project has seams, take care not to mash the yarn in the seam area, but do dampen the seam on the wrong side of the piece with steam or a spray bottle (according to yarn type) and gently finger-press the seam to reduce the bulk. This also serves to set the seaming yarn and prevents the yarn ends from working their way out.

TASSELS

SUPPLIES

▶ Combination of coordinating yarns (no specific gauge or type)

▶ Cardboard

▶ Scissors

▶ Tapestry needle

DIRECTIONS

1. Cut cardboard 1" longer than the finished length of the tassel. Place all yarns in a basket, shopping bag, or box. Take 1 strand of each yarn and wrap them all together as one around the cardboard square. Count the number of wraps as you go (in the event that you want to duplicate the tassel, you will need to know this). Wrap your yarns at least 25 to 35 times—you want a fat tassel! Cut the wrapped yarns along the bottom of the cardboard square and place the lengths of yarn flat on a table.

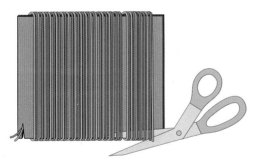

2. Make a twisted cord about 20" long (see page 92), and place the cord flat on the table. Take your cut yarns and place them on top of the cord, making sure the yarns are "centered" on the cord. Then tie the ends of the cord firmly around the yarn once.

3. Fold the cut yarns in half with the twisted cord at the top and wrap the "neck" of the tassel with one strand of the yarn that you have used in your tassel. Hold this strand along the side of the tassel and, starting at the top of the neck, wrap the yarn evenly and tightly around the neck. This secures the tail and becomes a part of the tassel. Thread a tapestry needle with the opposite end of the yarn and go back and forth through the neck of the tassel several more times. To secure this end, go one half of the way through the neck of the tassel and then down through the center of the tassel toward the bottom.

4. Hold the tassel in your left hand and cut the strands of yarn evenly across the bottom.

5. Steam the tassel over a teakettle, holding it with tongs. This will smooth and fluff the tassel. Use a crochet hook to tie the ends to your pillow or throw.

TWISTED CORDS

SUPPLIES

▸ Coordinating yarns used in or complementary to throw or muffler

▸ Cup hooks

▸ Hand drill with a cup hook in the bit

▸ Fishing weight with a curtain hook in the loop

DIRECTIONS

1. Select your yarns and decide on the desired length of your finished cord. Multiply the finished length by 4 to get the correct length of the fibers. Use approximately 10" of twisted cord to attach tassels. Make enough twisted cord to cut into several 10" lengths (see step 9 at right). You may combine several strands of your fibers (these can be all the same or coordinating fibers). The thickness of the finished cord will depend on the number and type of fibers chosen and the end use of the twisted cord itself. Experiment to find the thickness you desire.

2. Holding combined fibers together as one, tie a knot in each end of the combined fibers.

3. Place a cup hook in a doorjamb or doorframe at approximately waist height from the floor. The drill has a cup hook in it already.

4. Loop one end of your fibers over the hook on the door and the other end in the hook of the drill. Holding the drill, stand far enough from the door to maintain tension in the fibers.

5. Twist the fibers by winding the drill, counting the number of times you wind as you go (you will need this information in the event that you want to duplicate the twisted cord). Some combinations of fibers require more winding than others.

6. When the cord draws you toward the doorframe as it shortens due to the twisting, it is almost ready for the next step. To check the tension, take hold of the twisted cord 6" from the drill, maintaining firm tension between the doorframe and your hand. Let the tension "relax" slightly between your hand and the drill; the cord should twist into tight knots if the cord has been twisted enough at this point. If more winding is needed, remember to keep track of the number of winds.

7. Holding the drill in your left hand, take the weight in your right hand and place it in the center of the twisted cord. Keeping the cord taut, place both ends of the cord on the cup hook attached to the drill. Hold the drill up so that the weight twists freely. When it has stopped spinning, remove the weight, take the two ends off of the cup hook in the drill bit, and knot the ends together to secure the twisted cord.

8. To finish the cord, put one end back on the doorframe hook and the other on the drill hook. Reverse twist the drill 20 times. Take the cord off of the drill hook and let it unwind. This takes the bias out of the cord.

9. To attach tassels with twisted cords, knot the long cord as shown and cut between the pairs of knots to make shorter cords, approximately 10" long.

Cut between knots.

FRINGE

This is a basic description for adding fringe. You may select one yarn or a combination of yarns held together as one, depending on the look you prefer for a particular project.

SUPPLIES

- Yarn(s)
- Scissors
- Crochet hook to accommodate yarn(s)

DIRECTIONS

1. Cut strands of yarn(s) twice the desired finished length of your fringe.
2. Fold the strand(s) in half and, using a crochet hook that comfortably holds the size and quantity of the yarn(s) chosen, insert the crochet hook into the edge of the throw 1 st above the CO or into an edge st from front to back.
3. Loop the fibers over the hook on the back side of the throw and pull to the front, leaving half the length of the fibers on the back of the work. Put 2 fingers through the loop created by pulling the fibers forward and pull the ends of the fibers from the back through this loop. Pull firmly to secure.

4. Repeat this procedure at even intervals across the length of the edge that you want to fringe.
5. Trim fringe to a consistent length.

SNEEZES

This is our name for the small tufts sometimes added to a throw for extra fullness where fringe or tassels are attached. See "Naturally Neutral" on page 28.

1. Using the same materials as for fringe, cut yarn(s) into 3" lengths.
2. Using a small bundle of the 3" lengths, place yarn(s) at the point that each tassel is attached and, using a crochet hook, pull a longer strand of yarn or silk ribbon through the throw from front to back; tie the ends of the longer strand to secure the sneezes in place.

TRICOTER SPECIAL SERVICES

It is our commitment at Tricoter to offer the most luxurious, unique fibers and ornamentation available in the European and domestic markets and to assist you in the design and creation of your own one-of-a-kind, hand-knit garment or home accessory. Tricoter offers complimentary design services and guidance through the completion of projects to all of our customers. We believe that it is the detail and finishing that elevates a garment from "loving-hands-at-home" to a beautiful hand-knit original. Therefore, we offer a variety of classes from basic skills through advanced techniques and finishing.

Because we realize your time is precious and limited, Tricoter is also pleased to offer a variety of custom knitting and finishing services for those occasions when you require professional assistance. We have a number of out-of-town customers with whom we work on a regular basis to assist in the completion of hand-knit garments. The following is a brief outline of our services:

▶ Expert finishing services are available at an hourly rate. You can turn your work in progress over to us at any stage.
▶ We offer a variety of custom knitting services for your convenience. All garments are individually fitted and beautifully finished. We will work with you to design and create a sweater, jacket, coat, or home accessory of your choice that reflects your individual style.
▶ We have one of the most extensive collections of the finest hand-painted needlepoint canvases, fibers, and accessories available in the Pacific Northwest. We offer both individual and small-class instruction for needle-work, and professional blocking and finishing for all of your needlepoint projects.

We have an appreciation for beautiful fibers and fine design, and we share our expertise and assistance with you—from the selection of fibers to a design that reflects your individual style. Please feel free to contact us for additional information regarding any of these services.

Tricoter
3121 E. Madison Street
Seattle, WA 98112
Phone: 206-328-6505
Fax: 206-328-0635
Toll Free: 877-554-YARN
                 877-554-9276
E-mail: tricoter@aol.com
Web: www.tricoter.com

BIBLIOGRAPHY

Fassett, Kaffe. *Glorious Knits.* New York: Clarkson N. Potter, Inc., 1985.

Square, Vicki. *The Knitter's Companion.* Loveland, Colo.: Interweave Press, Inc., 1996. The best "carry-along" reference book we've found. Small, sturdy, light-weight, and very complete.

The Editors of Vogue Knitting Magazine. *Vogue Knitting.* New York: Pantheon Books, 1989. *The* comprehensive source to your hand-knitting questions in easy-to-understand language with clear, concise illustrations.

YARN RESOURCES

For a list of shops in your area that carry the yarns mentioned in the book, contact the following companies.

Colinette
Unique Kolours, Ltd.
1428 Oak Lane
Downington, PA 19335

Filatura di Crosa, S. Charles Collezione, and Tahki
Tahki-Stacy Charles, Inc.
8000 Cooper Avenue
Bldg. #1, Third Floor
Glendale, NY 11385
info@tahkistacycharles.com
www.tahkistacycharles.com

Hanah Silk
Artemis Exquisite Embellishments
179 High Street
South Portland, ME 04106
www.artemisinc.com

GGH, Horstia, and Horst
Muench Yarns and Buttons
285 Bel Marin Keys Blvd., Unit J
Novato, CA 94949-5763
muenchyarn@aol.com
www.muenchyarns.com

Ironstone
Ironstone Yarns
414 Bibb Industrial Drive
PO Box 8
Las Vegas, NM 87701
jemmott@newmexico.com

Lang
Berroco, Inc.
14 Elmdale Road
Uxbridge, MA 01569-0367
wwheelock@berroco.com

Noro, On Line, Gedifra, and Euro
Knitting Fever and Euro Yarns
35 Debevoise Avenue
Roosevelt, NY 11575-0502
webmaster@knittingfever.com
www.knittingfever.com

Prism
Prism
2595 30th Avenue North
St. Petersburg, FL 33713

Rowan
Westminster Fibers, Inc.
4 Townsend West, Unit 8
Nashua, NH 03031-2335
wfibers@aol.com

Trendsetter
Trendsetter Yarns
16742 Stagg St. #104
Van Nuys, CA 91406